WISDOM
in the
WAITING

**Other books in the
Stories from The Farm In Lucy series**

What the Land Already Knows

The Graces We Remember

Stories from The Farm In Lucy

WISDOM
in the WAITING

Spring's Sacred Days

PHYLLIS TICKLE

LOYOLAPRESS.

CHICAGO

LOYOLAPRESS.

3441 N. ASHLAND AVENUE
CHICAGO, ILLINOIS 60657
(800) 621-1008
WWW.LOYOLABOOKS.ORG

All Scripture quotations are from the King James Version of the Bible.

"Final Sanity" has appeared in a number of publications, including *The Tennessee Churchman*, for which it won the Polly Bond Award in 1985.

"Garden Myths" appeared as "Of This April's Showers" in *The Episcopalian*, as has "Ascension Day" in slightly different form.

We are grateful to each of these publishers for the use of the materials reprinted here.

Cover and interior design by Megan Duffy Rostan

Library of Congress Cataloging-in-Publication Data

Tickle, Phyllis.
  Wisdom in the waiting : spring's sacred days / Phyllis Tickle.
    p. cm.
Rev. ed. of: Final sanity. c1987.
  ISBN 0-8294-1765-6
 1. Lent—Meditations. 2. Easter—Meditations. 3.
Eastertide—Meditations. 4. Farm life—Religious
aspects—Christianity—Meditations. I. Tickle, Phyllis. Final sanity.
II. Title.
  BV85.T49 2004
  242—dc22

                                  2003016860

Printed in the United States of America

04 05 06 07 08 09 10 11 M-V 10 9 8 7 6 5 4 3 2 1

Contents

Prologue

Homemade stories, my late mother-in-law used to say, are really just facts that people own in much the same way that they own any other part of their household goods, all of which are a little overvalued, a little ragtag around the edges, and a little antique in form. Once was the time I acknowledged Mamaw's observations as folksy, if not downright quaint. Now that I am as old as she was then, I know better. Folksy and quaint or not, her analysis is certainly true. (There is, of course, a lovely irony in my having discovered no readier way to open a book of homemade stories than with the tale of a matriarch's insightfulness. My matriarch would probably have regarded this as more curious than quaint, however, for she was a staunch realist who brooked no romanticism and little self-indulgence.)

This, then, is a collection of facts that have been owned down into stories, Lenten and Easter stories that are more accurate, perhaps, and more possessed now than they were even when I first wrote them. I say this because, by the grace of God, the young lives—mine and Sam's as much as our children's, children-in-law's, and first grandson's—whose progress is captured here in still-frame have gone on to mature in the ways of the heart, the body, and the land. In our growing we have carried these spring tales with us, most of us to places other than the farm, but each of us has continued to catalog and edit them as one does a library of heritage and identity.

In 1976, when our country was celebrating America's position of wealth and world dominance almost as much as—perhaps even more than—it was celebrating the hardtack independence that had been our founding, Sam and I finally found the courage to confess to each other what we both had known for several years. Both of us had been born late in our respective parents' lives. Both of us, as a result, had been reared by a generation whose youth had been spent more in fields and barns than in groceries and dry goods stores; and also as a result, both of us had been taught by unspoken and unselfconscious, albeit exquisite, daily example how to grow and tend, make and make do.

What he and I confessed to each other in the autumn of 1976, then, was that not only did our children have none of these skills, but they also possessed none of the freedom or the discipline that come from knowing how to live with and on the land. Ultimately, it is always the land and what it knows that sustain life; and it was to the land that we had to take them before it was too late. So with five of our seven children still at home, we began to look for what Sam described to the realtor as "adequate acreage and a solid barn with a useable house somewhere on it." That phrase probably said it all, for the next year we signed the paperwork on The Farm In Lucy without his ever having been inside the useable house. It was sufficient to his way of thinking that the barn was incontestably solid and that the pastures would sustain at least two-dozen head of cattle.

Lucy, Tennessee, if you should ever chance to come here in person, is only about twenty miles due north of Memphis, Tennessee, and twelve or thirteen miles, as the crow flies, from the eastern banks of the Mississippi. In 1977 it was also separated from Memphis by at least a hundred years. A town that had devolved into a village that, by the time of our coming, had devolved into a community, Lucy had once been a thriving stop on the Illinois Central Railroad. As Memphis had grown, however, the pull of commerce had shifted south, leaving Lucy as a quiet little village with a couple of general stores, a fine old school, and about four thousand citizens if, as we used to say in town meetings, one counted the tractors as well as the cows and people.

The pull now, of course, is in the opposite direction; and as the city spreads closer and closer, the number of people goes up as the number of tractors and cows goes down. Thus even now we still number about four thousand in aggregate, but we count ourselves in souls these days rather than resident entities. We have only one general store on Main Street, though it is by common agreement the best we've ever had; and we still have the state's most accommodating old country schoolhouse, despite the fact that it suffered the insult a couple of years ago of a totally utilitarian addition on its back side. The community church whose bell, in our early years, tolled the village's dead as well as our worship, is now a wedding chapel that tolls nothing, for its steeple and bell have long since been removed.

In all of this change, Sam and I have changed as well, of course. The Farm In Lucy—as our children and their children call it now, complete with capital letters—The Farm In Lucy is hardly a farm these days except in memory. No herd grazes here, no horses are stabled here, no crops grow, and this year no garden was even planted. Common sense would say that we are too old to want the responsibility of such, and common sense would probably be right; but more to the point, common sense also says there is no need any longer. The lessons have been taught, the gifts given, the children reared. What the land teaches has passed on to them. That part of it is done.

Sam and I spend a good deal of time these days praying that the children and their children and, now, their children's children will keep the faith. But as surely as the original writing down of these Lenten and Easter stories was a way to forestall any forgetting, the retelling of them here has been, for me, part of this new way of praying. And in the certain knowledge that family prayer is best said in community, I hope you and yours will join me and mine in this one. The latchstring is out on the door at The Farm In Lucy.

CHAPTER 1

No Palms in My Purse

It was a long time ago, and half a lifetime of experience. In early May, Nora had gotten married. Our oldest, she was the first of the children to leave us and, according to her father, far too young to have any notion of what she was about. Being quite old enough to know exactly what she was about, she had ceased to argue the point with him and had proceeded, with all due respect and decorum, to get herself married anyway.

By late June, and with the wedding bills all paid at last, Sam was still disconsolate and out of sorts because of the hole in his life. I decided it was time to do something—anything—to shake up our routine and interrupt the apparently interminable period of paternal mourning. A vacation seemed in order.

It is a fair measure of my concern that I even mentioned such a thing. Rebecca, our seventh and last acquisition, was not quite two, and the other five still with us were scattered, at various levels of the humanizing process, between her and their now-missing sister. And I *hated* family vacations!

At that time in our lives and for obvious reasons, we owned one—actually we had owned and worn out a couple—of those huge overland Travelalls that International Harvester used to make for folks with our kind of problem. This particular Travelall, however, was still fairly new, and it was certainly still roadworthy. Granny, who lived with us, could no longer sustain the two days of hard driving that lay between us and Florida's Atlantic coast, but I could take her and Rebecca down by plane. Sam could take the other five children with him by car, and we would meet in Orlando.

The sea had always—in the days before children— revived Sam and me. Surely it would do so again. Beginning the trip at Disney World would set just the right tone of excitement and adventure for the children and would make them weary enough to enjoy the simpler life of sunning and swimming, which Sam and I wanted. At least that was the theory as I proposed it to Sam.

Physicians—my physician husband anyway—don't take many vacations. They may leave town for those seminars and meetings that are necessary to keep them abreast of developments in their field, but neither Sam nor either of his partners was ever enthusiastic about being gone for very long. It was a measure of Sam's doldrums, therefore, that he even listened to my proposition. But he did. And once the idea had been stated out loud, like an evil weed it not only grew but refused to die.

For one thing, in a house with six children and a grandmother, even words shared in the dark of midnight behind the closed doors of the upper bedroom are heard. They are whispered through the walls and into the hours of the early morning. By noontime they are disseminated, and by twilight they are fact. It was so with our vacation. At supper the evening after I had mentioned the idea to Sam, Granny was telling him that two weeks in Florida was exactly what we all needed. He looked accusingly down the table at me, and truly innocent of the charges, I simply shrugged. He shrugged back. We were going on vacation.

It took three weeks to arrange the excruciating details of how Sam would leave behind the hospital and his patients. Who would cover which night was hard enough to establish; the long hours of consultation over patient charts, worrying about who might possibly get in distress were impossible. Listening to it all, I remembered why we never took vacations anymore, and it wasn't just having all those children and a grandmother!

Finally, having managed to arrive at the hottest part of July, we also arrived at the appointed time for leaving. Sam was to pull out on Saturday morning with the Travelall, our gear, and the kids, if he could get them in. Granny, Rebecca, and I would follow on Sunday afternoon. It was, therefore, late Friday afternoon when Sam discovered that, if he got the suitcases, cameras, makeup kits, potty-chairs, floats, books, and coolers into the Travelall, he, in fact, really couldn't get the kids in.

He made a hasty trip to Sears just at supper and spent fifty desperation dollars to buy what Sears called, rather inelegantly, a "clam shell." The contrivance was hinged, tracked to sit on top of the luggage racks of big station wagons, and designed to hold everything you ever wanted with room left over for what you could never, ever have need of.

What Sears didn't tell you, of course, was that once you got the thing in place, got it stuffed, and lashed it down, you couldn't open it again until you got to where you were going—not, that is, unless you wanted to unlash, unpack, and unload the whole thing all over again. Since this rather obvious point had not been immediately apparent to us, Sam did have to unlash, unpack, and unload just before ten o'clock that Friday night. He showed, I must say, a remarkably negative attitude about the whole thing at the time.

By six o'clock Saturday morning, however, after five hours of muttering sleep—he muttered and slept; I lay beside him and listened—he was ready to pull out with his part of our ménage. He had all of the kids except Rebecca, or at least he said he did. I couldn't see any of them through the windows because of all the floats and makeup kits and pillows he had had to retrieve the night before. But at that point I was willing to take his word for everything, and he was in no mood to be crossed. So he pulled out, leaving me thirty-six hours in which to prepare my soul for the ordeal ahead—gird up my loins, so to speak—and to repair the damage Daddy and company had left behind.

At not quite two, Rebecca still had a vicious case of that perfectly normal malady—the favorite-blanket syndrome.

Hers was not a blanket actually. Hers was a wondrously soft patchwork quilt that Mamaw Tickle had fashioned for her out of scraps of old velvet. It was also huge, hot, and filthy—velvet won't wash or even dry-clean very well. And there was no way Rebecca was going to leave that house, much less get on that airplane, without her quilt.

By three o'clock Sunday afternoon, when our plane had missed its connection in Atlanta and we had to be shuttled in an open cart across the tarmac to the flight Eastern was holding for us, I had developed a strong dislike for Rebecca's equally strong quilt. It had been all over me, the flight attendant, and Granny on the late flight in. Now, in the July heat of central Georgia, it was wrapped solidly across my shoulders—the only place I could carry it while holding on to a toddler and a grandmother—as our driver careened his way over the perspiring asphalt. By the time we finally deplaned in Orlando, the quilt was thoroughly moist with not only the sweat of my brow but also the end results of a too-long-unchanged diaper. But at least we had no trouble finding more than enough room to ourselves in the back of the motel's airport shuttle. Things were looking up.

By six o'clock a bedraggled Sam was parking the Travelall outside our door, and shortly thereafter our three rooms were threatening to burst. Granny had been assigned the peaceful room with Laura and Mary. Philip had been appointed overseer of the boys' room and Daddy and Mama had drawn Rebecca and the quilt.

All three rooms had adjoining doors, so the relegation of goods and people to a particular room lasted only about five minutes. Besides, the Travelall travelers were much too hungry to be interested in unpacking. The last of the suitcases were simply shoved in our door. Just as Sam was locking the door behind us, I thought to open up Rebecca's quilt and drape it over the pile of luggage to air and, I hoped, to dry. Sam locked up and we left.

Dinner, as best I can remember, was one of those unmemorable affairs one feeds children on the road— lots of hamburgers and French fries and calories—but it was refreshing, as were the laughter and silliness that went with it. We really had done the right thing to come after all. I felt a sense of relief that it was all going to work out—and the vague hope that the quilt was dry enough so that Rebecca could go right to sleep with it as soon as we got back to our rooms.

After dinner, and with ice-cream cones in hand, we headed back to the wagon and the motel. Sam was even singing—always a sign of serious well-being—when he unlocked the door for us.

"Oops! Wrong room!" he said, chagrined, as he backed out and closed the door before we could even see in over his shoulder.

He looked at the key, looked at the number on the door in front of us, looked up and down the line of closed doors on either side of us, shook his head, and looked back at the door.

"I don't understand. It's the right number."

He inserted the key and opened the door again. This time we all crowded in behind him. The room looked just fine to me. Just like the one we had left . . . but not just like we had left it! Except for the usual furniture, there was nothing in it! No luggage, no coolers, and no quilt!

There had to be a mistake. The motel must have moved us while we were at supper. Sam went to the phone to call the desk. Philip meanwhile went into the boys' room and announced that everything there was just as they had left it. There couldn't be a mistake. Laura, in turn, discovered all of the girls' gear still in place in their room.

The young lady at the front desk was as surprised as we were. It took no more than two minutes, however, for the manager to make it out of the office and around to our room. He was *not* surprised. They had had a rash of break-ins the past two weeks, apparently a disgruntled former employee trying to ruin the motel, taking everything, even the silliest things ("Wet baby quilts, for instance?" I asked), more to anger patrons than to steal. In fact, they had found some of the suitcases in the dumpsters around town. The upshot was that the manager was very sorry, a condition no one was denying him at that point. The motel would of course like to have us as its guests without charge for our stay and would make such restitution as it could of our goods, a point that Rebecca began immediately to deny him, for it was at that moment that it dawned on her what had happened.

She howled, and the beleaguered manager, having said all he could say, backed his way toward the door, assuring Sam that it would be easier for everyone—he nodded in the direction of Rebecca and me—if the two of them were to step down to his office to call the police and complete the necessary papers.

Mary astutely took Granny to bed, and Philip discovered an absolutely compelling cops-and-robbers show on the boys' TV. Both had the charity to leave their doors open, should I get into real trouble, but neither offered much encouragement beyond a knowing shake of the head.

The howling diminished to wails, and the wails were interrupted with "I want my quilt," but there was to be no ready diminishment of her grief. I could hear the sirens downstairs in the parking lot, and through the crack in the drapes I could see the blue lights flashing. Three cars. Poor Sam. He could be at this all night. Rebecca wailed. Poor me. I would be at this all night!

During the next half hour I rocked, Rebecca cried, and Sam Jr.—just-turned-five and always the tender one in the family—wandered wistfully back and forth between our two rooms. He stood finally in the doorway between, watching Rebecca with a distress on his face as real as that which she seemed to be feeling. From time to time, he would come to us, stroke her face with his pudgy, little-boy hand, and then leave. He never told her to hush or that it would be all right. Stranded in that space between his own babyhood and the boy toward whom he was growing, he still remembered his own quilt. Of all of us, he most knew that it would indeed not be all right.

Sam came back, tired, frustrated, but in good humor. It had happened, and it was over. His concern now was all for Rebecca and/or getting everyone bedded down for a big day tomorrow despite her distress. I rocked and he marshaled, so that in a relatively brief time all was quiet, save for the sniffling baby in my arms. He lay down, and in the quiet, Rebecca began to croon, "I want my quilt, Mommy, I want my quilt. I want my quilt, Mommy, I want my quilt," over and over.

"Hush, now, baby. We'll get you a new quilt. Mamaw will make you a new quilt."

"I want my quilt, Mommy, I want my quilt," as if she had not even heard me.

"Mamaw will make you another quilt, baby. Go to sleep now, and tomorrow we will call Mamaw to make you a new quilt."

"I want my quilt, Mommy, I want my quilt."

"Mamaw will make you a quilt. . . ."

"Don't tell her that." Sam Jr. was standing in the dark just inside our room. "It won't do any good. A new one won't have her dreams in it." Then he was gone, a little piece of boy in white underwear and no pajamas.

I rocked on after that until the crooning stopped and Rebecca drifted, weary beyond even her own grief.

The next morning all was sunshine and Mickey Mouse. We called Mamaw, and either Rebecca understood what we were doing, or she was simply resigned. She whimpered at naptime and again at bedtime, but the wailing was over and the vacation, so eventful in its beginning, was almost ordinary in its ending. Fully rested and revived, we returned, two weeks later, to home and a waiting parcel that held a smaller, more hastily made, but nonetheless velvet, quilt from Mamaw.

Sam Jr. was right, of course. Rebecca watched as Mary unwrapped the box and lifted out the new quilt. She took it and smiled as she buried her face in its softness. She even sighed as she slid off my lap and snuggled down on the floor with it. But it was almost a year before she loved it—before she had put enough dreams into it to need it.

It was almost ten years, though, before Rebecca's blanket took on its final meaning for me. Sam Jr. was fourteen then, almost fifteen, and taller than I, but still the tender one. Almost to manhood and strong as his father, he stood sometimes, more than any of the others, in that space between remembering and growing.

Each year on Palm Sunday, before we begin the final hymns of the Triumphal Entry, our priest elevates the palm fronds that have been used to decorate the altar, blesses them, and hands them to the ushers. As we pass, singing, toward the front of the nave, each of us takes and carries out onto the parish lawn a single frond. When the hymns are done, the procession finished, and the benediction shouted above the chatter of the birds and the excitement of the children, we go our separate ways, each carrying a frond into the coming year. I carry mine—as I always carried the children's, too—in a pouch in my purse. There, from time to time, I sometimes deliberately seek it; and there, by its mere presence, it will from day to day remind me of why I am here . . .

. . . until next spring when, as they do each year on Quinquagesima Sunday—the Sunday before Mardi Gras and Ash Wednesday—the women of the altar guild will stand near the church door, their hands held out to take back our palms from the various pouches and pockets and Bibles where we have harbored them for almost a year. The minute I see them standing there, I am filled with the desire to turn back or to slip by, to not let go of my frond this year. Tuesday, in this same building, it and all the others like it will be burned, their ashes saved against the coming of Ash Wednesday services. From Quinquagesima Sunday until Palm Sunday, though, I will have no palms at all. Because I am not yet old enough to be candid about such things, I turn my frond in as dutifully as I always have. I go away saddened by a loss I will not feel again until next year and of which I will not be entirely relieved, even on Palm Sunday when I receive my new frond.

This loss became particularly clear to me that year when Sam Jr., more than fourteen and not quite fifteen, still wanted to keep his palm frond for himself. He and I had agreed between us that it was time for him to accept the ways of Mother Church. When we came, then, to Quinquagesima Sunday the following spring and the waiting altar guild ladies, I watched as he pulled out his frond from the shirt pocket under his sweater. He hesitated before he handed it over. When he realized I had seen him, he ducked his head. "It's a lot like Rebecca's quilt," he said by way of apology. "Full of dreams."

Well, I thought to myself, *I didn't know he had remembered after all these years, but I certainly should have known that he understood.*

CHAPTER 2

Mardi Gras and Other Portals into Mystery

M ardi Gras has always seemed to me to be one of the more stellar examples of the church's wisdom. While most of us in this country know the day by its French name because of the New Orleans experience, its English name is equally engaging, at least to me—Fat Tuesday—and certainly reflects most accurately its immediate, physical result.

In the old days before adequate refrigeration, the Christian wife had to arrange, on this last day before Lent, the total consumption of all the delicious and sinful foods in her larder. (We are talking here about pure country butter, sage-laced sausage, and moist lumps of brown maple sugar, among other delectables.) They had to be either eaten or destroyed before Ash Wednesday came. The result was one of the world's most incredible feasts, and any nutritionist will tell you what all those calories in one day will lead to: drinking, dancing, and riotous living.

On Fat Tuesday still we symbolically lay away the foods of rich energy and begin the next day on a lean diet of bland restriction, the purpose of which is to—in the coming weeks of Lent—better taste and know our God. When I was an undergraduate, I was taught in some psychology class that the most definitive difference between a philosophy and a religion is that the latter requires the eating of the atonement sacrifice, while the former is revulsed by such notions. It was a hard distinction for me to understand as an adolescent.

Mardi Gras, with its carnival and its homage to the pagan, is the church's recognition of how our faith must develop. It is also a recognition of the spiritual necessity for primordial darkness, and of the uses of the other side of light. It is our chance to remember, one time a year and with sanction, the long way of our coming and the strange way of our arriving. In its own way and when combined with faith, it is one of the most instructive holidays of the church's year.

All of us who arrive at spiritual maturity do so by moving through a progression of faiths and comprehensions. In much the same way, all of us who now walk had first to move through a fairly unoriginal progression of motor skills before we arrived at our walking. In effect, what the spiritual process leaves most of us with is a veritable pantheon of early gods and codes, discarded in our maturity, but essential to our growth—gods and understandings that led us to Easter in the first place. In just that way, and on the farm, my children were first introduced to mystery, not by the Church's feasts, but by a furnace named Beelzebub and a bedroom wall we called Stonehenge.

Our only near neighbor put in a wood-burning furnace one year, an incredible contrivance whose like I had never seen before and whose functions proved to be a source of constant family conversation for years. The furnace itself, a freestanding box of sizable proportions, was situated—or, as the children would say, got plopped—on our side of our neighbor's house where we could, with delicacy and complete discretion, watch every part of its installation. Of course, we continued to watch every part of its use as well, also with complete discretion.

The best we could tell from our vantage point, the air thus heated ran through an underground pipe over to the central air conditioning system where, by some method never apparent to one husband, two sons, and three sons-in-law, the central air motor and ducts conveyed it into the house for circulation. Not being mechanical or even bent in that direction, I cared not at all about how the blessed thing worked, but I was fascinated by such juxtaposing of central air conditioning and primitive heating. I was also downright entertained by all the ways in which primitive heating could command the energies of its owners.

The first thing we noticed was that an electric light had been strung out the kitchen window and attached to the body of the furnace. It took two nights and one late trip to the hospital for Sam to discover that the lamp was there to illuminate the furnace's 2:00 A.M. feeding. I could remember that light helps in such matters.

The next thing was that the neighbors' tractor, which had heretofore always been carefully parked in the lean-to of the barn, now stayed out all the time in the side yard beside the furnace box. Apparently pulling the flatbeds of wood up to the box and pulling ashcans away from it became a frequent enough event to discourage even Mr. Fleming from parking and unparking the tractor half a farm away. *Interesting*, I thought every time I watched yet another load of wood being brought in and left just beside the furnace door.

By early December of that year, our first truly cold month with the furnace, Mr. Fleming had begun to show a serious interest in pruning his trees. The first ones to go were down in the back pasture, and they probably really did need to go. But when he started topping an oak in his front acreage, the children whooped and Saturday lunch was delayed for an hour while they watched the process.

Country children or not, our youngsters were each and every one dedicated to creature comforts, and electric heat was number one on their list of creature comforts. Sam, in contrast, had long been notorious for his attempts to remain ecologically in balance, by which he meant independent of outside sources for our necessities. Apparently the near presence of yet another method of being ecologically balanced seriously threatened the children's sense of well-being, especially the boys', who could foresee hours of chopping and loading should the

Flemings' monster prove workable. This final evidence of kinks in the scheme of things delighted them beyond anything that year save Christmas itself.

After the oak topping, they were free to both observe and comment with impunity. There was, in particular, considerable wagering one winter on whether Mr. Fleming would leave the thing in place once spring finally came, or whether he would retire Old Beelzebub (their name) to the nether reaches from whence he had come. So in the weeks of that March and April, as the days grew warmer and the evenings less and less chilly, I found myself more anxious about, than interested in, Beelzebub's fate. It was an enormous relief to me, then, when Mr. Fleming had the generosity not only to leave Beelzebub in place all summer but also to fire him up with the first chilly evenings of the next fall.

Over the dull months of two winters and the long weeks of one Lent I grew accustomed to Beelzebub, maybe even fond of him. His smokestack, which sat no more than three feet high, constantly emitted a lazy spiral of smoke that was not unattractive in and of itself. In addition, the odor of the burning wood was so pervasive as to scent pleasantly every part of our house. It was rather like living in a Christmas-card world all winter actually, and I would have missed it had Mr. Fleming shut his contraption down prematurely.

But mainly I would have missed Beelzebub's information. Unlike the children, I was at home all day, my office window looking right out into Old Beelzebub's face, and I came to count on him as thermometer, windsock, and snow gauge. In our almost two winters together, he was never wrong. When the stack bellowed with smoke, it was too cold to go out without a shawl or wrap. When the smoke blew north toward the Flemings' orchard, it was going to be sunny. When it blew south toward the highway, it was going to be much colder before suppertime. And, alas, when it blew east toward us, anything could happen, and whatever it was, neither we nor the stock were going to like it much. The happiest choice for me, since I was a child at heart, was for the smoke to crawl out of Beelzebub's stack, hesitate, and then slink down the box, hurrying away just above ground level. That meant snow, and I felt as giddy as the Cumaean sibyl telling her vapors when, at twilight, the wet flakes began to fall.

Obviously all this same information—and with almost the same degree of accuracy—could be got by listening to our NOAA station or by tuning in to the evening television news, but I was like Sam. I liked to stay ecologically balanced. Besides, Beelzebub was a much more romantic prognosticator than NOAA, in addition to being easier to consult. So, subtly and noon-time by noontime, Beelzebub stole his way into my affections and my habits, and I was honestly glad of his survival and ongoing good health. He became part of our scheme of things, rather like Stonehenge.

"Stonehenge" was Sam's name for our bedroom. The room itself was originally two rooms, both of them adequate but apparently inelegant in size. At some point some previous owner had taken out the separating wall and created a space more comparable to a double garage than to a bedroom. The resulting space had one window facing east by northeast, two facing east by southeast, and two facing almost directly south.

The first year of our living here, I luxuriated in the spaciousness of our quarters—this was what Mama had always meant by *master bedroom*—and the glories of the southern windows. Every plant or flower or vine that I set in front of them would instantly respond by thriving to incredible lushness and vigor. There was nothing in the plant world that could not be revived or nursed back to health by a week in the bedroom windows! But while

I was busy puttering with plant life, Sam was busy with other matters.

It was during our second winter here that he began curiously to make marks on the western—and only solid—wall of the bedroom. Lying in bed in the mornings in the soft time between waking and rousing, he would roll over toward the wall and, with his finger, make a faint smudge on the white paint. Then he would get up and set about his chores as if nothing unusual had happened. It was the third week of June that second year and the morning after the summer solstice when he first said, "Stonehenge!" Actually, he woke up, rolled to the wall as usual, and then exclaimed, "Aha! Just as I thought. Stonehenge!"

Over the winter months his smudges had progressed northward along our western wall to its farthest point at the head of our bed and around the corner onto the northern wall against which the bed sits. But this morning the next-to-the-last smudge, which Sam had made two days before, was glowing in the slit of early morning light that came in around the shades. Even befogged by sleep, I could still share his excitement. By removing the wall, someone before us, either knowingly or accidentally, had created a highly accurate astrological device. And Stonehenge our room has been ever since.

While no one would ever find our bedroom wall more useful than the almanac, or even more accessible in this case, and while even Sam confessed that this was carrying ecologically balanced living a bit far, there was something very comforting about knowing that we could calculate without a calendar. There was also something very intellectually reassuring about knowing, from personal and diurnal experience, the awe of the ancient mysteries. What the books related about the Druid priests on the Salisbury Plain was nothing compared to the emotional effect of watching Sam's sliver of light move each winter north up the room and then, turning, come back south to the middle of the wall by Christmas.

More than that, of course, there was the immediacy of Old Beelzebub's smoke and of Sam's smudges, which granted the children the grace of unstudied knowing and a direct but mysterious connection with seasons and solstice. Stonehenge and Beelzebub became portals for them, just as the original Stonehenge and tales of Beelzebub had been for the ancients. And just as a closet had, once upon a time, been for me.

Huge in its dimensions and cavernous with its ten-foot ceiling, that closet of my childhood was a city one. Full of mothballs and almost-dispatched toys, it was redolent with the scents of my mother's perfume, cedar boxes, and my father's collection of newspapers—one for every day of the Second World War from Pearl Harbor to Hiroshima. Everything in that closet was planned and preserved for its utility. Even the shelves were so spaced as to make an uneasy ladder up to the forbidden trap-door that opened onto insulation and crawlspace.

From the first beginning of conscious memory, I had arranged and stored myself in that closet. I was the one who threw out its excess, wrought order upon its collections, and sorted its debris for the raw materials of my soul's education. Whatever parent or cousin or time dumped out, I sorted by feel in the dark or by stealth with a flashlight, spiriting out the useless to the alley trash bins and climbing to the top-shelf repository with the remains. There neither my short-of-stature mother nor my taller-but-less-inquisitive father ever could or would go.

The closet was a pantheon for my childhood's gods. It was as full of personalities as was my father's copy of the *Inferno*, illustrated by Doré and secreted years before on the upper shelf, much to my father's recurring puzzlement. The upper shelf's walls sang with awesome pictures of Shiva, Astarte, Hecate, and so forth, all torn from the pages of my grandmother's discarded *Chamber's Illustrated Encyclopedia*. A china Ferdinand the Bull, which my uncle had brought me from New York, shared the closet's fantasia with crayoned tracings of satyrs much less benign than those Walt Disney would have wanted me to believe in. And the arms of the goddess Kali (brass and beautiful from India but repugnant to my mother, who had thrown her away) waxed over the whole of the shelf in constant incantation.

Somewhere just near the attic crawlspace was God the Father, his beard frequently no more than a cobweb, but still he was there—or passage to him was. Even as a child I knew that there was no God the Mother and was glad. I did not want one. Gentleness, nurture, support, stroking were sexless in my understanding, belonging to neither gender exclusively and to both identically. It was Kali with her many-handed sexuality whom I wanted as the Queen of Forever. It was Kali who helped me hone the diffuse appetites of youth into focus.

Kali was the only one of the closet's treasures to escape its destruction. She alone still sits on my bedroom dressing table. All the rest have long since gone as

victims to my own maturing or the house's new owners.
I threw Shiva and Astarte away before I was fully ten
years old. In high school I had to study Dante and, for
convenience, moved him back down to the more accessible bookshelf. Doré's ghouls and phantasmagoria by
that time were more eternally etched into my faith than
they ever could have been into the pages of any book.
Ferdinand I had broken one adolescent day by hurling
him against a brick wall. In a rush of need to know what
it was to kill someone I truly loved, I had hurled him
away from me. Even today I can still feel the slick heat
of him as he slid from my hand to his multifaceted
destruction. Like so many toys for so many children, he
served me better in death than in life, and I never
mourned him. Bit by bit and doll by doll, the other
treasures were carried out and dispersed to other children, to nieces, nephews, neighbors, some even to my
own children.

During Vietnam and not long before his death, my
father burned his World War II collection. It was after
his funeral and before we sold the house that I finally
moved Kali out of the closet and to her place on the
dresser in Stonehenge. Somehow she seemed more
beautiful to me there than ever before, as if being once

more part of a pantheon for imaginative children were her real purpose in this life.

Pancakes and sausages and carnivals. Fat Tuesdays and ash-marked Wednesdays. Earth time caught in calendars of light and dark beyond human control. Winds and weather read by smoke. Many-handed creatures dancing in fluid pose. These things are the stuff of mysteries, the stuff of the dark, enticing, luminous dreams through which we have come and to which we cannot quite return. They are evidence and agent of a knowing we half remember from childhoods and have half inherited from the genes of our forebears. They are the romance of religion, its texture, the surety that holds the soul in the spirit's dance, and nowhere are they richer or more present for me than in the dusky, brooding days of early Lent.

CHAPTER 3

Of Swallowtails
in Particular

The last chores of the day were always bathroom chores for me—collecting all the wet towels and shucked underwear for one last trip down to the laundry room; rubbing on the cleansing cream that felt cold even in the summertime and then rubbing it and my makeup off again; rinsing one last ring out of the tub before I crawled in myself for the warm soak that eased my body into sleeping and my day into summary.

I suspect, truth be told, that the bathrooms in a lot of houses function in the same way that ours did—that their principal function has never really been the declared business of cleanliness and hygiene, but rather privileged solitude in the midst of intimate community.

In the early days when there were many of us at home, however, the bathroom was the prize as well as a sanctuary. If you got up early enough or stayed awake late enough, you had a chance of getting a bath instead of a shower. With any luck you could even wash your hair at the same time instead of having to hang your head over the mop sink in the laundry room later.

Like all parents of many children, Sam and I have spent our fair share of time hiding in the bathrooms of our various houses. Some of my most credible thoughts, certainly, have come in those midnight tubs when everyone and everything, including the last of the hot water, had gone away for the day.

But our crowding and our need for sanctuary changed over the years. Our early years on The Farm In Lucy consisted of a family of five at home. We had three bathrooms: one for Sam and me, one downstairs for John and Sam Jr., and—luxury of luxuries—one for Rebecca all to herself. It was her bathroom that most persuaded me that overcrowding and overactivity were never the real reason for our bathroom retreats.

Becca did everything in her bathroom; half her day-time life was conducted from there. She painted for hours on end—all over the farm—but the lab in which the paints were both mixed and stored was her bathroom. A perfumer at heart, she had, ever since she could reach the bathroom sink from her little wooden step stool, mixed the petals of every flower she and her father grew. She soaked them for days in concoctions that only the two of them knew, because Daddy was the one who, up in her bathroom, showed her what glycerin would do, and alcohol, and even beeswax and lanolin. When she was ten, her experiments into the essences that could be thus extracted and/or suspended would have done honor to a much older practitioner, and her ongoing pleasure in her experimentation was so pervasive over the years that I tolerated the mess in fascination, cleaning around, rather than through, it.

Originally the perfuming began as a result of flower collecting. By the time she was six, she simply could not let the flowers die in the fall. More and more of them were picked and brought into the bathroom to be cajoled into extended life by every means she could contrive. At first she simply made crude pomanders, which always molded. By the time she was eight she had managed to assemble three flower presses in the bathroom: one she annoyed an older sister into buying for her, one she made for herself by the simple process of nagging

John until he cut the boards and drilled the holes for her, and one she got by default when Laura married and moved away. In just a few months after that last acquisition, she progressed from pressing to drying and from drying to preserving. Mason jars of noxious deterrents to vegetative death lined the tile floor in front of her shower stall so that, while taking a shower was still possible, climbing back out was a definite hazard.

All of which would have been domestically tolerable if the function of her bathroom hadn't moved from flowers to creatures. At first it was daddy longlegs, which was fine and even normal. (After seven children I regard daddy longlegs all over one's bathrooms as almost ordinary, in fact.) Then it was praying mantises, which was sort of on the money, too. Then we got to the snails— twenty-two of them at one point—also in the shower stall. There seemed to be no real reason for having collected them. They were just there, rather like Mount Everest to a climber. But observing them must have conveyed something, however subliminal, to Becca because the next summer snails were replaced by caterpillars.

There was none of the true biologist's absorption in cataloging and categorizing. Not with this child. Any caterpillar would do, just as long as it crawled and was stupid enough to be outside when Becca was. At age ten—which she was when this particular wave of perversion overtook us—she wasn't even enough of a student to consider the probability of stingers, and she paid for that a time or two. Whatever else she may have learned or not learned from the summer of the caterpillars, she surely learned which ones not to harass, at least not with her bare fingers.

The captive caterpillars were all housed with a kind of naive abandon about natural sympathies and animosities. As a result, I have to report that some of them were eaten by others of them, but the Mason jars that had previously held the noxious chemicals were once more lined up in front of the shower stall, filled this time with caterpillars and eventually with cocoons.

There is a kind of phlox that looks a bit like butterfly bush but seems to be more nourishing. During those years, Rebecca and her father grew the stuff in every available inch of flowerbed around the patio and along the back of the house. It allowed them to entice dozens of hummingbirds near the windows of the kitchen where we ate. The bumblebees were intoxicated into apparent ecstasy by the pollen. But it was the butterflies that proved to be incredibly varied and numerous in their feedings. Sometimes in the late afternoons of July and August, all of the patio beds appeared to be on the wing, so great was the activity.

It was, naturally then, the phlox that Rebecca decided to feed to her caterpillar horde. Day after day that summer handfuls of the purplish stalks went through the kitchen and up the hall to the bathroom. Day after day I followed behind her, picking up a trail of fallen purple petals. From the back door, through the kitchen, and up the stairs to Becca's room I went twice a day, complaining every step of the way about kids and their messes, all the while wondering to myself whether I was indeed soft enough and traditional enough to be putting up with all of this simply because she was the baby and I was going to miss having children around. I finally decided that I was and that I would. It was a depressing discovery after all those years of saying, "I can hardly wait, Lord! I can hardly wait!"

The caterpillars, meanwhile, were fed unreal amounts of phlox, and those that weren't themselves eaten all thrived. In fact, just going into Becca's bathroom got to be a scary thing. The boys, who in the past had rather resented her status of single owner and had pestered her frequently for the right to use her shower on hot evenings, gradually lost all interest in even try-ing to get in. The rewards were totally canceled out by the experience of having all those jars of crawling eyes see you buck-naked—or at least that's what John told me one night when I asked him why he didn't use Becca's shower to clean up anymore.

So the summer waned into fall, and the fall showed every sign of waning into winter, and the cocoons came. Now the jars were full of depending paper sackettes. This thing was getting interesting even to me. To everyone's amazement, including my own, I cleared off the back of the toilet and made a kind of shelf for the jars so I could see them better. I think I also had some notion that the light and the cycle of day and night might be essential to the proper development of what-ever it was that happened to a pupa, but I would never have admitted to Rebecca that that was my motivation. I simply claimed parental weariness, saying that all those jars made mopping the floor impossible. At this point, the tile floor really had achieved an impressive layer of purple rot in front of the shower door.

The winter came and left. Then, in mid-April, we discovered that while Rebecca might not have been much of a cataloger of collections, she had nonetheless stored in her head a complete inventory of which caterpillars had made which cocoons.

"What do you mean, that one is going to be a swallowtail?" I asked her one afternoon in amazement when she moved one of the jars downstairs into the kitchen so we all could watch it.

"Well, I think that's what it will make." She was answering me with less sureness than she usually had when challenged. "It had those two sets of dark hairs like a swallowtail should have when it's a worm."

I knew I probably wanted to let that one alone, but she picked up a pencil anyway and drew me a picture of the caterpillar she had captured, saying, "See, this right here should become this right here," and the bug sketched into a butterfly under her pencil.

"I'm not sure it works that way," I objected.

"Neither am I. That's why it's down here."

By the afternoon that the thing finally hatched, I was prepared to be all emotional and motherly about the event. Rebecca came in from school to the jar and the emerging butterfly I had been watching for the better part of half an hour. She sat down and began to observe the last stages of the process without a word. *Well*, I thought, *let her alone. She'll talk when she wants to* (never a problem with Rebecca), and I went upstairs. In a little while I heard the back door slam and then slam again. The water went on in the kitchen, and I couldn't stand it any longer. I went down, and there she was, washing out the jar.

"What happened?" I asked.

"I let it go. It was a swallowtail just like I thought—had to be because of the markings. Stuff like that doesn't change just because you can't see it."

She could not have been more indifferent. I have always questioned all the butterflies on church bulletins and Easter cards, and I have doubted, even more, all the butterflies that get hung about in some kind of anxious homage to a vague hereafter; yet I simply could not ignore this child's cavalier treatment of the biggest cliché in popular religion.

"But, Becca, the caterpillar died to make that butterfly! Don't you think you should at least care a little bit about that?"

She shook her head. "No, ma'am. I think that whatever died, died so the markings would live."

She started drying the still-cloudy jar with my clean tea towel. "The markings were what mattered. They made it a swallowtail," and she walked off, carrying the jar with her back up to her bathroom. I rehung the rumpled towel and forgot about Becca and the swallowtail . . . until Ash Wednesday.

Ash Wednesday was probably the one day in the Christian year that ever bothered our children. The thing itself was fairly simple. The palms they loved carrying in procession the year before on Palm Sunday had been burned to make ashes, and those ashes were then blessed before Ash Wednesday began. Whether we gathered at the 7:30 service in the morning, or at the midday service, or as occasionally happened, when we attended the evening service in order to all be together, the end result was always the same.

We moved through the prayers and readings as if this were just any other day of the year until, following the communion, the congregation returned to the altar rail for the imposition of the ashes. Putting his thumb in the small dish he carried, the priest moved in front of us, making the sign of the cross on each forehead.

It was (and remains) the only time of the year that we were ever marked, that on our bodies we carried the sign of the faith. Both ancient and primitive, the marks would stay with us throughout the day. It was always the manner of a child's acceptance of the sign, then, that told Sam and me where that child was in understanding what it meant to say, "I am Christian."

That year, Ash Wednesday began early for us: up for 7:30 services and the ashes that were drawn black and heavy across my forehead. But that night, as I reached for the cleansing cream, my prayer was simpler than in years passed.

"Father, let Becca be right. Let me have been about the markings all along."

CHAPTER 4

Watching and Waiting

The sky was petulant when we got up that morning, churning itself above us, as heavy and pulpy as papier-mâché. Even while I did my morning chores among them, the animals were as silent as the day, their conversations limited to Alouette's mew for her kittens and an occasional cry from the drake. In the far pasture I could see the cows herded against the close, half of them still standing lest they be caught unprepared by what they were restless to hear.

The hours of our early morning had all been used up now in our waiting. Knowing better, and more from habit than wisdom, I sat down at my desk, pretending to myself that I would work awhile. Instead I stared out the window. I watched. Like the cows, I feared what we were waiting for.

A draft from off the river, ten miles to the west of us, moved across the yard. It tossed Sam's forsythia bushes and lifted his holly branches momentarily. In what seemed like delight and false relief, my favorite wood-pecker sailed from one pine tree to another. But the wind died, and he once more assumed his silent posture atop the new tree. He, too, was waiting, and I pondered, disinterestedly, whether or not the grubs he usually heard in the pine bark were also silent that day, whether they, too, were waiting.

Water began to drip off the corner of the gutter and down into the flower bed—condensation too cool to make rain, too sparse to find the downspout. Finally, as if shamed by his own fear, Dublin rose stiffly to his gatepost, hesitated, and at last sounded the day. The hens followed his noise into the fowl lot, pecking and scratching without enthusiasm as they came. Seeing them below him, Dublin escaped from his perch into the freedom of the farmyard.

Two butterflies began mating above the kitchen flower bed. One by one, they were joined from nowhere by five more. The guineas came wandering up the path from the orchard, beeping and barking crossly as they came, and the ducks rose, in a hurry suddenly to get to the feed trays beyond the patio before the guineas did. As always, the ducks lost, giving up the race with angry quacking and agitation. Like a great patriarch, Dublin tried to scold them all into silence, but to no avail. Neither guineas nor ducks would be instructed by a chicken, not even by one who was a friend.

Abruptly from across the fields I heard a motor—a tractor, probably—kick off and begin to drone. I sighed with relief. So many times before I had seen it all happen, had witnessed this subtle end to waiting, that I knew by heart how the rest of the day would undo itself now. Shortly the cows would change their position from the close to the open hillocks above the pond; the woodpecker would hear his grubs at last and go after them; the phone would ring. I started back toward my work.

The yellowish gray outside my study windows began to lift itself away. Already the trees beyond the fence were clearer. Soon they would be florescent in their greening bark. As I talked to some man on the phone about why we didn't want solar heating installed, or whatever it was he was trying to sell, I could see the trees begin to move comfortably again, their tops bending, ever so slightly but ever so consistently, back and forth in the breeze, which must have come up just as I began talking. The phone call ended, I began to move through the house, closing windows, grateful that, in the final analysis, today was still too cool to make the tornado we almost had.

Somewhere upriver the weather that had passed over us would be shaped by the heat of the late winter earth, would focus, and would destroy with a fury increased by our having denied it. Dublin crowed again, I assumed for the sheer raucousness of it. Even he must have known by then that no one was paying him any mind at all. The sun came through the trees, its light winking at me from the water troughs. Our tornado had indeed moved beyond us.

In my sun-bright office with a breeze lightly singing in the eaves above me, I sat back down and played in my mind the footage we would see on the television tonight: the leveled trailer park, its pieces strewn across perfectly flat land; the aerial shots, including the especially long one of a shopping mall missing its roof; at least one tree-blocked section of interstate, and, of course, one broken and discolored doll caught on the jagged edge of wreckage.

That's where our storm had gone—where it had been carried by our sophistication. I had lost it already in the predictability of the package by which it would be returned to me. In the inevitability of its targets. In the clichés and maudlin metaphors of its about-to-be television life. Somewhere upriver, in western Kentucky or southern Illinois or central Ohio, someone would have a bitter afternoon, have individual reason to remember that day for the rest of time, and I could only think of, not feel with, them.

All the natural and cultivated barriers that information could throw up against emotion rose now to insulate me. So much space and so many differences of circumstance protected me. Even memory refused to relieve my impotence, and I, listening now to my woodpecker hammering away for his grubs, could no longer feel how viciously his silence had oppressed me not thirty minutes ago. I could remember only that it did.

Pain in all its forms—loss, grief, depression, agony— is much too intense in its presence and much too unimaginable in its absence for any of us to have many pretensions about it except to know that it is the one barrier that really does separate us. It is the impassable moat that surrounds each person's castle and denies entrance to each person's center. Yet, that denial and that separation are themselves a kind of pain for those of us who wait outside the moat, cut off by it. Every Easter, as I look at the corpus on the cross above our altar, I am reminded of that separation, that inability to "know" another in pain, but I am also exhilarated by the promise that in resurrection I will know. The gift of Easter, beyond the obvious one of life forever, is the promise of life forever spent in praise and rejoicing and gratitude. Easter's great gift is an eternal consciousness that will know completely and will be able to celebrate in its entirety the price love has paid on our behalf.

CHAPTER 5

Final Sanity

The forty penitential weekdays and six Sundays that follow Mardi Gras and precede Easter are the days of greatest calm in the church's year. Since by long centuries of custom the date of Easter is annually determined from the first Sunday after the full moon on or after March 21, the intertwining of physical and spiritual seasons is virtually inevitable. The resulting union of deep winter and holy preparation makes reflection, even penitence, a natural activity.

One night years ago, toward the end of winter, there was a storm, a cold front shifting suddenly and dropping onto us with ferocity and winds that bent down the pine trees along the fence line. Sometime after I went to bed, it tore open the pasture gate. We awoke the next morning to bitter cold and a scattered herd: two pregnant heifers in the front yard, six more in the garden eating up what was left of the turnip greens, and seven others, mostly yearlings, playing at some kind of heifer tag in the windy orchard.

The mud from the previous month's snow was three inches thick. Even frozen, it came laughing up to suck off our boots. We slopped and fell and prodded swollen bellies until, ourselves covered with ooze, we fell onto the broken gate and laughed out loud to the gray dawn skies and the startled blackbirds. We drove the last cows through finally, my son John and I, and repaired the gate right enough, coming in out of the cold with feet so wet and frozen that we couldn't feel them, our night-clothes covered in the half-thawed manure. We stank up the kitchen with the good stench of late winter and of the earth when it is resisting one last cold front with the heat of coming fertility.

Later I stood at the spigot and washed the mud from our boots and felt again, as I do every year at this season, a grief for the passing cold. Looking across the pastures to the pond below, I knew it had indeed been the last storm before the spring, and I wanted to run backward toward the early morning, toward the winds and breaking limbs of the previous night.

"Lenzin," our German ancestors used to call this season, and since then we have called it "Lent." It is a time when Christians decorate stone churches with the sea's color and wrap their priests in the mollusk's purple. It was once a time when all things passed through the natural depression of seclusion, short food supplies, and inactivity, a time when body and land both rested. It is still, in the country, a final sanity before the absurd wastefulness of spring.

Each year at this time it is harder for me to desire butterflies and lilies, even to wish for resurrection. Each year I come a little closer to needing the dullness of the sky and the rarity of a single redheaded woodpecker knocking for grubs in the pine bark. Each year also I come a little closer to the single-mindedness of the drake who, muddy underside showing, waddles now across the ice to the cold center water to wash himself for his mate, all in the hope of ducklings later on.

That year, through the thin, sharp air I could hear the younger children in the barn. They were building tunnels again, making forts from the dried bales of hay. From the yapping I knew that even the dogs had joined in the intricacies that the children's imaginations had contrived. Five-year-old Rebecca chased field mice as her brothers built forts. She would catch another soon and drown it in the water trough with unsullied sadism, feeling only the accomplishment that came from having helped to keep her part of the world in balance.

In the summer, the mice would leave, going back to the fields again, and she would take to pulling everything that bloomed instead, bringing them all in to me indiscriminately. The tin-roofed barn would be stifling, and the hay forts would have all been eaten. The boys would be picking beans and complaining of the itch from the okra leaves, being themselves too hot and tired to desire anything except nightfall and bed. The drake would have a family, which he would abandon to the mate he had so much desired, and the woodpecker's carmine head would burn out to tired tan.

The farm in the summer becomes like the city is all year: too much color, too much noise, too much growing, too much hurry to stave off loss and destruction, too little natural death and gentle ending, too little time for play, too little pointless imagination.

I can remember many summers now; it is the singular advantage of years that one can do so. And I remember that once summer comes, I spend it wallowing in the easiness of it—the excess of its fruits and vegetables, the companionship of summer's constant sounds as the hum of the insects and of the rototillers give way in the evening to the croaking of the frogs and the raucousness of the katydids. I remember also how I would begin early, in that green time of Ordinary Time, to dread the stillness of the coming cold, to fear the weariness of winter menus, the bitterness of breaking open pond water for thirsty cattle, and the packing of lunches— interminable lunches—for reluctant children on their way to school.

But now, years later, it is Lent once again, and for one more snow I can luxuriate in the isolation of the cold, attend laconically to who I am, what I value, and why I'm here. Religion has always kept earth time. Liturgy only gives sanction to what the heart already knows.

CHAPTER 6

On Just Such a Morning

There were no walls to experience, the farm inside me being always larger and freer than the one that lay waiting outside my kitchen window. I was my own window that morning, and I came to my prayers like Janus looking both ways . . . outward to where Nimrod the mighty cat stalked the patio in pursuit of a guinea chick he didn't really want, and inward to where a thousand equally casual deaths and near deaths had blended into acceptance and peace in the balance.

Dublin the rooster stood tall on the gatepost of the chicken yard. During the winter that had preceded us, he'd lost his comb to the bitter cold, having preferred the pain of frostbite to confinement in the hen house.

Now, crownless except for his scar of black and withered skin, he swayed from his perch more vigorously than he had when he was whole. This too I brought in to me, this regard for scars and purchase.

The early spring crowded around us—around Dublin and Nimrod and me. It waddled with the ducks crossing the greening yard toward the fowl lot and scurried with the guineas in their frantic discovery of the missing chick. It grew deeply and insistently up the kitchen window toward me, vining and budding as it came, but I would have none of it. I'd not be so easy a convert to merriment that morning. Too many beginning springs had seduced me before that one.

Beyond the fence line, Flash, the gelding, moved away from the mares to look across the yard, an immense air of tragedy pervading the whole of him. He stopped briefly to neigh toward the kitchen door, lowered his head to scratch his neck along the cedar railing, and moved on. He had no prayers standing between him and his ordinary habits—no interior pasture in which to feed—and I was glad for the simpleness of his purpose, the directness of his life. Mine was not so— certainly not that morning, when I walked two lands, the one that I housed, having been built of daily pieces from the one in which I was myself housed.

It must have been on just such a morning as this that the young Mary first was told, first knew that she stood between two worlds, and "was troubled at his saying" (Luke 1:29) . . . and across the intervening centuries I reached out to her fear and reverenced her confusion.

Below me on the patio Nimrod tried again for the chick, but this time the cock was there. It was over in less time than it took me to laugh—the cock on the cat, talons burying deep in fur, beak pecking hair and drawing blood, fur and feathers intertwined and racing across the patio and into the low-lying holly bushes, Nimrod scraped free of his burden by the low-lying prickles, and the guineas on patrol around the bed. Even Flash had turned back to watch, and Dublin, ever a gossip, crowed his delight from atop the hen house roof.

It was all too much for me, and I was at last seduced. I went out into the farmyard, adding, as I went, its frolic to my prayers. Of these things, too, is worship made.

CHAPTER 7

The Bleeding Birds

Not all of the creatures in our lives have been subject to domestication, even on the farm. Some of those most central to our experience have also been the wildest, like the egrets, for instance.

We first saw the birds—we think—in the fall of 1978. There's no way now to be sure. Back then we didn't record the farm's naturally occurring fauna with the same care that we used to track the equipment and the stock. I wish we had. But at the time we thought they were just cranes that had, for some unknown reason, come farther inland than usual from the Mississippi.

Mary saw them first and came running. I was upstairs moving winter clothes out of the hall closet and getting ready to carry them out to the back clotheslines to air when she came charging up the stairs, saying, "This you won't believe!" and ran beyond me toward our bedroom and her father's binoculars.

Actually, they were Sam's only in name and in place-ment. They had once been one of his proudest—and, I might add, most expensive—possessions. That was in the city. They had also been one of the few things unequivocally denied to children and usually to spouse.

Country living, with its myriad excitements and thousand wonders had eroded Sam's proprietary posi-tion down to having the things still referred to as "Daddy's binoculars" and to a firm rule that, when not in use, they were always to hang in their case from the large loop of his tie rack, securely shut within the con-fines of his closet. He frequently and bitterly mentioned to me that all that this had accomplished was to remind him of the days when he had once been in control— that, and to keep his ties in an eternal jumble.

But while he was away fighting bacteria and neu-roses, I was left on the home front, and riding shotgun on his binoculars, much less his ties, had just simply been beyond me. Consequently the children—espe-cially the older ones, like Mary, who were essentially grown—had long since given up even saying what they were doing as they headed toward their father's tie rack.

When she emerged from our bedroom, therefore, I knew without looking what Mary had gone in for and what she had come out with. I met her, as a result, in our bathroom.

Our bathroom, long since a failure as a bathroom but a huge success as a family room, enjoyed, among its other questionable assets, an absolutely unequaled view of the back ten acres of the farm.

We met at the commode and the window above it. She was right. It didn't even take Sam's glasses for me to know what she had seen and to agree that no one was ever going to believe it.

The whole back pasture from the fence line halfway to the cattle pond was white with them. And they were moving as the sea moves, in undulations, curves, lifts, and falls. Never had I seen such a thing. The sheer magnificence of their whitecaps on our stubbled hay was beyond my capacity to react to. I stood stunned into silence by the sensuousness of their movement. Neither of us said anything for a full minute and a half, maybe two, before I understood that the children also had to see. "Call them to come quietly," I whispered to Mary, and she nodded and went.

They came—loudly until they saw—and then they too stood silently as they gathered, one by one, in front of the window. The pasture beyond us continued to roll and rise, lift and resettle.

"May we go out to them?" It was John who was so hushed by what he was watching. At eight he was the one least likely to be quiet, much less to speak with precision. Looking down at him, however, I realized that he needed to go out among the birds.

"Yes," I answered, as softly as he had asked.

But while the rest of us watched, the birds, as if sensing his approach, lifted one last time, hundreds of them, and moved westward before the boy even got downstairs, much less out of the house.

The next time they came, there were fewer of them, and it was almost winter. The wools and corduroys had not only been aired and hung into our respective closets; they were being worn again. We watched the birds with just as much excitement, perhaps, but with a great deal more skill.

Laura and John and I stood in the bathroom and watched. The birds showed less restiveness, and we dared, all three of us, to open the back door and walk out toward them. We eventually made it to the fence without alarming them, and we stood watching for maybe a quarter of an hour. We could see enough of their features to realize that whatever they were, they weren't cranes.

It would be almost three years later, when the birds had become a three-or-four-times-every-fall part of our lives, that John, still absorbed by the meaning of them, would finally come home with proof of their identity. They were cattle egrets. *Scientific American* or *National Geographic* or *Smithsonian* or some similar publication said so.

John brought the magazine home and laid it open in front of me on the kitchen counter when he came in from school one day. "Look what I found," he insisted, and there, in the current issue of whatever, were our birds, along with a six- or seven-page essay about the miracle of their arrival in North America.

The cattle egret is indigenous to Africa, where it has apparently lived for centuries. For some reason, the birds had begun in the 1930s to migrate. According to this article, they had made it into the Mississippi Valley in 1977.

Reading John's magazine, I was awfully glad that we had been visited by the birds for several seasons before he found the footnotes that explained and validated them. Miracles, in general, suffer a certain loss of poetry when they become certifiable. The children seemed to agree with me, although I suppose in fairness to science I ought to confess that it was nice to know what the birds really were, and it was rather exhilarating to know that we had a world-class miracle, or at least a media event, in our pasture.

But the birds, either because of the consistency of their fall appearances or because of the article or because of that demon, familiarity, became less important, less startling, over the years.

It was two or three years later, after we had grown more careful of our details and more proprietary toward our miracles, when we saw the birds for the first time in spring rather than summer. I was sitting at the kitchen table paying bills when, for some reason, probably fiscal distress, I turned around in my chair and looked out the picture window behind me toward the pasture. There, high in the dead oak that stands in a small close at the upper end of the pasture, was a wounded egret.

His breast was covered in blood, and he appeared to be too weary or weak to do anything except cling to his perch in silence. He was, even in his distress, incredibly arresting, more breathtaking, in fact, than I could remember the birds ever having been in the past. I could not decide whether it was the April light, the sight of this bird alone, or the abnormally heightened yellow of his comb that accounted for his great beauty, but passionately beautiful he was.

It was already midafternoon, and I quietly put my work away and gave myself up entirely to watching the injured egret. He moved not at all. He did nothing. Unlike the usual pattern of lifting and resettling that the birds had always followed before, this one either couldn't or wouldn't move, much less fly. He simply hung there high in the dead oak.

In a few minutes, another egret flew in and settled wearily down on an adjacent limb. He too had been injured. He too was bleeding through his breast feathers. *Enemies?* I wondered. *Mating rivals who had fought earlier in the day and had met here to complete their contest? If so, neither seemed to have the strength or the will to continue their battle.* I began to wish for the children to come home.

Just before three o'clock the first school bus pulled up, and one by one we became a family again. Beyond us in the pasture the egrets began to assemble also. By three-thirty there were seven of them in the old oak, each one of them commanding in its beauty, each one possessed of a brilliant yellow comb, and each one bleeding across the whole of its chest and lower body. None of them moved.

Either these were birds who fought in a very consistent and destructive manner, or something else was happening here. I theorized out loud that even ritual fighting would allow some variation in the wound sites. And fighting to the point of such bloody results seemed incompatible with the kind of longevity and strength it takes to migrate from one continent across a major ocean to another continent. We all agreed that the whole thing didn't make sense.

Finally, I did what now seems to have been the logical thing, but which at the time seemed almost silly. I picked up the phone and called the municipal zoo in the city and asked for the ornithologist on staff. The ornithologist on staff, whoever the poor soul may have been, was plainly not accustomed to getting calls in the middle of the afternoon from John Q. Public, and especially not from Mrs. John Q. Public. "You have what?" he asked me again.

"I have a tree full of wounded egrets," I repeated.

He started laughing. "Ma'am, do those egrets have red breasts, yellow combs, and acute weariness?"

"Yes sir, that's exactly what they have."

"What they also have is a high level of hormones," he chuckled. "It's springtime, lady, even in bird land," and he sounded like he was going to hang up.

"Wait! Can you tell me what they're doing?" (Stupid question, I realized, and started over.) "I mean, have they been fighting?"

That seemed to be a more manageable question. "No, ma'am. They actually don't seem to fight at all. The males just grow that comb and their chests turn red and then they sit somewhere while the females choose which mate they want, like a high school prom for birds, only in reverse."

"Well, they surely look like they're bleeding to death."

"Can you imagine a more appropriate way to go? Blood first, before the sweat and tears." He was chuckling again.

"No sir, I guess I can't," I said, and thanking him, hung up.

That night when all the excitement had died down and when each of us had relayed to Sam his or her own rendition of the bleeding birds, I repeated for him my conversation with the ornithologist, including the crack about the appropriateness of blood before the sweat and tears.

"Forget the sweat and tears," Sam responded sleepily from his side of the evening paper. "The guy is right. They're part of getting up every morning. It's the blood that seals the deal."

"You think so?" I was prepared, despite the sleepy voice, to engage in a meaningful defense of the primacy of sweat and tears in shaping life.

"Baby," he said, lowering the paper briefly, "everything we do in this life that we know, deep down in our guts, we can't ever undo, we mark first with blood, or holy water, or both. If you aren't old enough to know that yet, at least those birds are"—which, it occurred to me as he retreated back behind his paper, was as good an explanation of the difference between the sacred and the profane as I had ever heard. And the memory of blood-red egrets on a tree, I think now, is not such a bad image to hold close on the blood-red day called Good Friday.

CHAPTER 8

Runaway Son

Everyone has a "worst day of my life" story. Some folks I know even have two or three, and at parties can invent five or six more upon demand. I, alas, only have a "worst half-a-day of my life" story, and I have never told it before now. For one thing, mine doesn't lend itself to the usual conversation at social gatherings, and for another, it has no casual ending and very little humor to it.

We had been living on the farm for almost a year when it happened. It was early April, that brooding time when, as the poet Eliot says, God makes lilacs out of the dead December.

Anyway, the earth was brooding like any mother about to deliver, and it was my favorite kind of day, probably because I can empathize from so much prior experience. There was no sunshine as such, but a blanket of milky gray clouds through which the most electric and radiant of lights seemed to be seeping. The trees along the fencerow and down in the close, although they had not fully budded yet, were just green enough to catch the light and distort it into a kind of ghostly shimmer through which no breeze moved.

The older children were at school and Rebecca, who was three that year, was in her crib, settled in for a morning nap. Only Sam Jr. and I were up and about.

Even at not quite six, he was already my philosopher. Unlike John, who liked to roam the acres in search of whatever might present itself to him for his consideration or assimilation, young Sam liked simply to find a place and sit. Whatever came to him for assimilation was either noncorporeal or itself highly mobile.

His favorite sitting place was down at the pond; his second, down in the cemetery that abutted our lower pasture; his third, the magnolia tree in the front yard. The problem with the first two was that they were forbidden to him without the company of an older sibling, a restriction that somewhat compromised their function as places for effective rumination.

The cemetery was simply too far away for a five year old to go without supervision. Besides, there is a fairly treacherous bog between the pasture and the cemetery fence. As for the pond, it really was a bog—a deep, deep bog—as far as I was concerned.

Certainly the cattle moved in and out of it easily. (I had ascertained the gentle slopings toward its depths during the previous summer by watching how high in the water the cows stood as they came and went cooling themselves.) But I also saw, around its edges and down in its waters, the roots and limbs and plant life that won't restrain a cow but will drown a child.

The pond was the only horror for me on the farm, the one part of our world that had troubled my joy in being here. It had, in truth, brought me up wide-awake and with a pounding heart on at least half-a-dozen occasions since our coming to the farm. Always the dream was the same: I saw the face of one child or another, eyes open and hair floating, staring blankly up at me through the pond's brown waters. While some Freudian could probably make something of that, all I cared about was the reality of the terror the dream caused me—and the incontestable truth of the pond's danger.

Sam Jr. had always seemed to sense the intensity of my fear and the immutability of my rules. As a result, he had not tested them in the seasons we had been here. For my own part, I had bent over backward to see that some unwilling sister or brother had accompanied him to the pond at least once out of every two or three times he asked to go. So I had relaxed somewhat in the knowledge that we had a reasonable working arrangement held up by honor and good intentions at both ends.

Even at five he showed every evidence of being a good kid . . . sloppy beyond any hope of repair, absent-minded to a fault, and possessed of the family temper, but not rebellious. In fact, it was he who could always be counted on to do the kind thing, the perfect thing. The supportive gesture, the really intuitive drawing, the imaginative Mother's Day card always came from him. In return he really didn't seem to want much: some space, a chance to be left alone for a healthy hunk of his day, and an occasional audience for his long and detailed recitations of what he had seen and thought or almost seen and almost thought on any given day.

It was the long recitations that usually got to the family. After about ten minutes of listening—even of pretending to listen—to the exact process by which he thought the hornets probably make those nests and by which he proposed the next day to attempt a similar product, I wanted to scream. His sisters usually did. His brothers simply threatened him with early death.

On this particular morning, therefore, it was not unusual that he had followed every step I made from table to sink, from bed to bed, from bathroom to laundry room, demanding every motion or two that I "stop that!" and look at him while he showed me with his hands what he was trying to tell me with his words: about how he could take all the cedar posts left over from fencing the yard and haul them to the pasture to make a house, about how he could use the fence itself for the back wall of his house, about how he could roof it with some of the tin from the barn, about how he would have to move the extra bricks behind the shed to the pasture to put down for a floor, about how he would have to put the lawn chairs in front to keep the cows from knocking it down, about how . . .

Finally I screamed. Not loudly—Rebecca was already asleep by then—just emphatically. The best I could remember later, I said my share of devastating things about his longevity if he didn't hush right now and either go do it or quit talking it to death.

"Okay," he said with his usual cheerfulness when he was rebuffed, and out the front door he went. I do remember thinking it a mark of his fundamental good humor that he could always tell when he had pushed it too far and forgive us for our resulting explosions. But beyond that I paid him no mind. I did check once, a half hour or so later, to see if I could spot an area of blue denim blue in the top of the magnolia. I could and that was the end of that.

With Rebecca still soundly snoring that incredible snore of a three year old into serious sleeping, I went out the back door with absolutely no purpose in mind but to enjoy. That kind of day only comes about twice a year around here, and any other chores could wait for another, more mundane day. I sat on the back steps for a while feeling the life around me, absorbing the energy of the luminous light. Eventually I moved to the patio wall in order not to have even the house blocking me. The sense of air all around me was comforting, and I thought, as I sat there, that young Sam might just have come by some of his strange ways honestly.

Wouldn't it be nice to take him down to the pond for a little while, sort of as a forgiveness gesture for having cut his pasture house off so shortly? I checked my watch. Becca was good for another forty-five minutes at least.

I went around to the magnolia tree. No Sam Jr. I couldn't believe it! I looked again. Sure enough, the top of the tree was empty. I called. No answer.

He's begun his house, I thought, and went to the stack of leftover railings. No little boy, and no evidence that one had even been there.

His room, I thought, going back to the house. He wasn't there either . . . but his fishing hat was gone!

There was no way he could have made it to the pond without my seeing him from the patio wall—unless he'd slipped off deliberately out his bedroom door, around the house, through the orchard to the barn, and then down below the hillock. *Why in the world would he do that?* I asked myself. *To get there*, I answered myself. *To get there without being stopped.*

I could hear in my head all the things I had said to him less than an hour earlier, how I had sent him off to his own devices and told him—told him both sharply and sincerely—to entertain himself.

I made it to the pond without even stopping for my boots, slipping, sliding, and stumbling as I went. No

Sam Jr. I raced around the whole perimeter, damning the murkiness of the water and the eeriness of light. I could see nothing—absolutely nothing. The waters were impenetrable. *No. He couldn't be. He wouldn't have*, I told my pounding heart. I raced back up, calling, yelling, screaming as I went.

Gasping for air with which to call and still to climb, I made it back to the house. No little boy anywhere and no response to my calls.

The cemetery. Surely he was at the cemetery. But there was no way to get there and leave Becca. No way to go through the bog with Becca. I raced to the phone to call the only neighbors we had. *Thank God! The line was busy! Someone was home!*

As it turned out, only Bill Fleming was home, but it didn't take two seconds for him to look at me and know we were in trouble. He beat me by several minutes back to our side of the fence and was halfway to the cemetery before I got back to the house. By the time I had checked Becca once again and got back outside, he was coming back from the cemetery. No Sam Jr.

Then he said the thing we were both thinking. "Did you check down in the pond?"

"Yes." I could feel the tears of panic rising up.

"With a pole?"

"Oh, God," I cried, my recurring nightmare swimming in front of me. "No."

"Stay with the baby and keep hollering for him. If I don't find him, we'll have to call the sheriff." Then he added, "You'd best go call your husband." And he was gone, but in his bluntness he had put an end to all my agitation.

It had been almost an hour since I had last seen the spot of blue denim in the magnolia top, and well over an hour and a half since I had told my son to go away and leave me alone. A farm has lots of places to hide, but ours has none outside the sound of adult voices unless a little boy can't answer or won't. It was that simple. Whatever had happened had already happened. It could no longer be feared—it was.

I went in and called Sam, telling him what had happened, telling him he had better come, even telling him that I thought there was a good chance Sam Jr. had run away because I had refused to listen to him. "I'm coming," was all Sam said, and the line went dead.

Bill was right. I needed to go back to hollering, to doing something.

I went out the back door and turned my head to begin projecting my voice when I saw the streak of blue running a broken field through the pine trees along the fencerow, making for the front of the house. As he broke out of the protection of the trees and into the open space, I saw him clearly, the fishing hat still on his head, the jigs bouncing brightly as he ran. "Sam! Sam!" I half-screamed, half-commanded.

He stopped in midleap, saw me, and sank into dejected submission. He had made no more than two steps toward me before I had made it all the way to him and was holding him tighter than any child had ever been held before. "Baby, baby, baby," was all I could say and then the tears came. Convulsive, racking tears that only stopped when I realized that I was terrifying him.

When I finally managed to get hold of myself and look up, there stood Bill Fleming watching us, a dripping pitchfork still in his hand.

"I found him," I said feebly.

"I see," he said and waited for me to finish feeling along every inch of the little body I was holding, as if to assure myself through my hands that he was indeed mine again and all right.

When I was done and had sat the child back down, Bill said quietly, "Come here, son," and held out his hand. The boy went slowly, almost reluctantly, taking the proffered adult hand. The two of them went out of earshot and sat down together on the patio wall where, a lifetime ago, I had myself so peacefully sat. What they said to each other we never exactly knew, but Sam Jr. told us part of it.

After Bill had gone home, covered in our thanks, and after Rebecca was settled down with the afternoon edition of Sesame Street, Sam Sr., Sam Jr., and I faced each other over what was left of our lunches. "Why?" his father asked him.

"I don't know." He shrugged.

"Yes, you do know," Sam Sr. said.

Sam Jr. loves a story too well not to eventually give in, and besides, one of his stories had our total attention for the first time in days. "Because," he began, in that maddening way of his. "Because . . . well, because at first I didn't mean to . . ." Then it began to pour out of him. "I mean, I guess I didn't hear Mama at first, and then she was really mad when I did hear her. And I was scared to come. I was only in the garage anyway, and so when she came in the house, I went back to the magnolia."

"That was it?" I interrupted him without thinking. He had been so intent on his own story that my question seemed to disconcert him.

"No, ma'am." He shook his head as if remembering and then tried again. "When you started looking in the yard, I came back this way and hid in the well house," he said finally.

"That's where you were?" his father asked.

"Yes, sir. Until Mama went to the pond. Then I went back to the garage until she went to get Mr. Fleming. When she did that, I went to the shed."

I was stunned. He had watched every move I had made, countering each with a move of his own like two players in some kind of elaborate chess game. "Why didn't you just answer me?"

"Because," he said. "Like I told you. It was just fun at first, and then I got scared to come home." Suddenly the tears welled up in his eyes. "I was so afraid."

"Afraid?" I said. It had never occurred to me that there was any fear except parental involved here. "Afraid? What in the world were you afraid of?"

"I was so afraid you wouldn't find me and I would have to stay outside all night!" And he began to weep great, agonizing sobs of relief.

"You knew Mama would find you," Sam soothed.

"No, I didn't." He muffled his voice into Sam's neck as his father held and rocked him.

"But all you had to do was answer me," I protested.

The little strawberry blond head shook back and forth against Sam Sr.'s protecting chest a time or two before our son turned just enough to say, "I couldn't. You would've killed me if I'd answered before you got good and worried."

He was right, of course. One of us was going to have to bear the pain of our reconciliation and better me than him, at least from his point of view—probably even from mine, I finally decided, as I watched him snuffling up the last of his tears.

"What did Mr. Fleming say to you?" Sam asked.

"He said what I did wasn't funny, especially since I could really have been hurt or dead. He said you both love me an awful lot."

"Is that all he said to you?"

"Well," he cut his eyes up at Sam through long, wet lashes and grinned. "He also said he would personally beat my butt if I ever did it again."

"Good for Mr. Fleming." Sam was struggling to suppress an inappropriate grin of amusement and release. I was having the same problem at my end of the lunch table.

"Yes, sir. He seemed mighty sincere about it."

"I suspect he was," Sam managed to say without loss of sobriety.

"Yes, sir." And he went to fall asleep in front of Big Bird and the Cookie Monster.

But that night as, one by one, the others went to their rooms and to their beds, I delayed my own going. Even after Sam had finally gone up without me, I could not force myself toward rest. My gratitude for a child in every bed this night was cut through by my dread of what might lie ahead.

The dream of the child in the pond, while it had frequently disturbed me, had never been intimate enough to make me fear seeing it again. But that was no longer true. Now I understood what the dream was about. It was about guilt and absolute helplessness, and I could not commit myself to either of them again, at least not so soon. So I put off going to sleep until finally sleep would wait for me no longer. I drifted off in the easy chair where I was reading.

The next morning I awoke stiff but refreshed . . . and vaguely surprised. I rummaged through my memory for what was surprising me and recalled slowly that the dream had not come, or, if it had, that it had not awakened me, which is the same thing.

It really didn't matter much on that sunny morning in my easy chair whether or not the dream of the water-killed child was gone for good; it mattered a great deal that I had lived one night (and all the nights since, in fact) on the other side of it. It mattered, and still does, that that day on the patio when Bill Fleming, like some avenging angel in overalls, took a pitchfork to fish for my child, he pushed me beyond fear. He pushed me where women go so many times in our lives: into knowing that whatever is, is and that it must be accepted . . . that even the anguish it contains must be accepted.

But for me as for my runaway son. Coming in where the punishing imagination isn't needed but where the chastising process is sometimes is more terrifying than being left out all night with our dreams. Ironically enough, of course, it is Mr. Eliot of the December-bred lilacs—a poet, in other words, and not a priest—who talks about that kind of moving from nightmares into faith. He calls it death by water.

In the days before Bill Fleming and his pitchfork, I had always thought death by water was just a metaphor for Christian baptism. I was wrong, of course. Baptism is a metaphor for the passage. The Christian part is learning to call the other side "Father" and understand that as a title it too has been earned with agony—an agony we can name as Holy Saturday.

CHAPTER 9

Garden Myths

A long the edge of the front walkway and just to the inside of the curve where the flagstones turn to follow the line of the house, Sam planted a row of hyacinths years ago. They were, admittedly, not much as today's hyacinths go—a long way removed, in fact, from the lush Dutch imports in the yards and flower beds of most of our country friends. Each March and April they bloomed up shorter and more timid of color than most, and with blooms that only sparsely decorated the hesitant spikes on which they depended. But it was not for their flowerness that we had them.

They were Great-great-grandmother Gammon's hyacinth bulbs. More than a century and a half before, she had fetched them from Virginia to the Appalachian foothills in her own migration westward. Since then each Gammon child has carried them again as he or she left the home place to push farther on. For all we know, the bulbs may have originally been brought by the family from the other side of the Atlantic. About that the family records are vague, but we are very sure of the last 175 years and of the genealogy of the bulbs in this country.

Apparently Sam, in carrying the bulbs all the way to the Mississippi River, brought them farther west than had any other of Great-great-grandmother's descendants. He had, in keeping with family tradition, planted them inside the walkway curves of five houses and had four times dug them up again to make yet another move with us. And each time an older child has moved away from our house—or from any other in the family, for that matter—a clump of those special hyacinths has left in the moving van with him or her. So Great-great-grandmother's hyacinths bloom in dozens of yards each spring, making a chain of connection across the southern United States and nearly two hundred years.

What blooms every spring also is an understanding of what mattered in 1825. In a hard land with its scarcity of domesticated flowers, Great-great-grandmother must have seen in the hyacinths a portable symbol of her eventual victory over wilderness and enough promise of future generations that she built and passed on emphatically the ritual of the hyacinth.

But there may have been more to it than that. When I was a child growing up in the mountains of east Tennessee, the world seemed to me an insurmountable garden in which I was at best only a visitor passing through. The trees and the plants were pieces of the earth that rose and sank with the seasons and with the courses of their own life cycles, but they *were* the earth while I was only *on* it. It was a distinction that made the trees, in particular, seem to be more powerful and more ominous than any other part of my daily surroundings. They towered over everything we did. It was as if they were only waiting for us to grow weary or leave so that they could, with their shade and leaves and falling limbs and spreading roots, consume for the earth all that we had temporarily created on the surface.

I was never much of a flower lover, even in those days of childhood—at least not a grower and cutter of flowers. My joy was all in the open fields and hillsides where the flowers bloomed rampant and uncontrolled in a silly profusion of daisies and brown-eyed Susies. It was the Dutchman's breeches and the jack-in-the-pulpits hiding

beside the wild mountain streams that gave me pleasure. My father's yard and those of our neighbors
seemed then (and still seem) to be only extensions of
their houses, like rooms created outside of walls instead
of within them, rooms in which the furnishings are constantly being refurbished by planning and unrelenting
care. And since every season I knew that the earth was
going to win again by taking back to herself what my
father and our neighbors had so painfully put there, the
yards seemed to me no more than exercises in human
ego. They appeared to grow from the human need to
impose human will, however briefly, on the earth, in full
knowledge that we could never hold off the natural
chaos of vegetable life for long, that we could never stop
the preordained pattern of rebirth from dead forms.

So with the ignorance of a child I met the trees,
plants, and flowers as creatures whose life purposes and
cycles were superior to my own by virtue of their inde-
structibility and total mutability. What bloomed today
as a daisy would bloom next year as a sunflower or a
hollyhock. And I knew them all in the intimate way of
children. I found the king in the pansy bloom and
learned to make the morning glories cry out. I popped
the Japanese Lanterns and made shakers from the

poppy pods. But mainly I dealt carefully with them all. They were not my friends. They were mysteries set upon the earth as tokens, evidence of the need for caution, warnings to never forget that I was not of them.

It was natural to me, then, in my eighth year, when I discovered the ancient Greek legends, to understand the reverence from which the myths had sprung. What my elders called ignorance or superstition I saw as irrefutable and solid explanation. I wandered in my ninth year through a world of gods and demigods whom my father pruned, but whom I knew he would never discipline or shape completely to his will, whom I knew neither of us would outlive. It was a great joke I shared with the goldenrod and the pussy willow that they would live forever and we would not. The fact that Christianity later soaked through my understanding and forced me to change my notions of relative immortality never affected my love for the mystery of the myths, especially not the mystery of the hyacinth.

A most grand German lady who had known my family before World War II had given me a copy of *The Wonder-Book*. Leather-bound on deep boards and tooled by hand with gold letters and a gold Pegasus emblazoned across it, it was a treasure trove of impossible glories, the noblest of which were the myths of the plant world. And there I met Hyacinthus, the beautiful young mortal who was loved by the god Apollo. Hyacinthus was mortally wounded one day by a discus thrown by Apollo, and Apollo, knowing full well that creatures could never be immortal, could not save him. Instead the god quickly gathered each drop of blood as it fell from the boy's wound and planted the drops, one by one, in the soil of the playing court. From each drop of planted blood Apollo caused a flower to bloom, a bloom that, on each of its petals, recounts the drops of blood Hyacinthus shed and Apollo garnered.

As Hyacinthus lay dying, *The Wonder-Book* said, he uttered the mournful cry of universal human suffering, the high-pitched wailing lament of the dying—"*Ai–Ai–Ai–Ai*"—across the hills and valleys of Hellas. And as the blood of the slain boy bloomed, it bore in itself the written symbols of his dying sounds. For all the eternity that his flower life gave him, Hyacinthus would continue to spell with his petals the *A* and the *I* of his death cry. When I was eight, I didn't have to look at a hyacinth to know that every word of the story was absolutely true and that the strange two-petals-one-petal-two-petals-one-petal arrangement of each individual blossom spelled *Ai–Ai–Ai–Ai*.

The myth of Hyacinthus achieved heightened importance in our family early one February, when a neighboring farmer lost some of his unringed shoats. These young hogs rooted out from under his fence, as shoats without nose-rings will do, and appeared in strange places. One morning we woke up to a pond dam covered in Poland China shoats. One morning our near neighbors awoke to Polands in the barn. And one afternoon, while we were driving around the bend where the graveyard meets our property line, we almost had a sausage accident. There was no catching them. Then, a week or so later, I came home at the end of a tedious day in town to find three black-and-white Poland Chinas in the front flower bed, rooting and grunting away. Hyacinths have almost no nutritive value but an absolutely delicious taste. Cows have been known to drown trying to reach just a few more of the water variety, and pigs have an insatiable appetite for the earthbound ones. I knew, even before I had time to think it through, what had happened. I grabbed a stick and a son, and we set to. Never before have piglets suffered so much at the hands of so few. We stood them off for an hour and a half before Sam got home, and he and the owner recaptured them at last. But the damage was unquestionably done. The whole bed was a mud bath of turned soil and pig tracks mixed with frayed sticks and a little blood.

The younger children were solemn afterward, sobered by some sense of failure that they could not quite identify or define. Sam's distress was contagious. He knew clearly what had been violated. For days he left each morning by the front door, stood briefly in front of the trampled bed, sighed, and moved on to the car. The earth had defeated at least his small part of Great-great-grandmother's plan. It had simply reclaimed its own, despite five human generations. The almost two centuries of care that were success to us were nothing to the earth, and her patience had been as infinite as her victory.

Yet the unlikely and presumably impossible happened. It was on the rainiest day of a singularly rainy April when we found them . . . three stalks, shorter than most and more timid of color, the blooms only sparsely covering the spikes from which they depended, but they were there, three of them, a clump for each of the children who had yet to grow up and leave home. Rebecca, who at eight had grown up with a head full of Greek legends and family stories, pulled off a bloom—a single bloom—and set it on the supper table in a little dish of water. And across the fields of The Farm In Lucy, its six petals—two-petals-one-petal-two-petals-one-petal—spelled *Ai-Ai-Ai* in the yellow light of the setting sun.

That Sunday, as he did every year on Easter, our priest again cried out from the pulpit, "Death, where is thy victory!" But that year for the first time Rebecca would understand that at least the beginning of the answer to his question lay somewhere between Great-great-grandmother Gammon's picture on the front room wall and the mythical gods of Mount Olympus. It was her first lesson in serious religion.

CHAPTER 10

Father and Son

We were talking in the kitchen. It was Saturday just before lunch, and my hands were busy the way they always were when I was in the kitchen. It was this busyness of hands in peeling and cutting and washing that bought children time for talk, and it was easy talk that day. Sam Jr. was sitting on the kitchen counter, all six feet of him dangling and hanging with the same nonchalance of fifteen years before when I had first shown him how to sit there and hold on without falling. The countertop even had a crack in the front edge where his increasing weight had pulled it loose. I felt obliged from time to time to fuss at him for the crack that meant Sam Sr. would someday have to replace the counter, but he only said, "Aw, Maw!"

knowing I treasured the cracked counter far too much
to lose it for the sake of a more attractive one.

He kicked the cabinet doors with the heels of his
tennis shoes, swinging his legs and stretching that
incredible leanness of his. He knew he was beautiful, a
Greek god come to a Tennessee farm, and he played
his advantage as expertly as his baby sister played hers
with their father. He talked about the car he was going
to buy the next summer as soon as he had made
enough money. He rambled about the job he wanted
hanging sheetrock with a construction firm, and I
reminded him that he was the laziest child we had. I
also reminded him that his father was at that very
moment building shelves in the shop, an endeavor
with which he could probably be of substantial help.
He knew I didn't mean that either and didn't bother
to answer, only grinned. He had slipped away from the
shop and into the kitchen ten minutes before to have
this time over the potatoes, and he intended to have it.
He raised one leg laconically and set his heel on the
sink rim. I thrust my paring knife at his shoe, but it
bothered him not at all. He grinned again, and the talk
of cars became a kind of soft rumble in which I was

carried more by the music of his deepening voice than by his content.

Suddenly, without any preliminary break in his monologue, he vaulted off the corner of the counter and threw himself half across the kitchen. Taking the steps three at a time, he was down to his room and back again. He raced by me and out the kitchen door. I heard the gun before I could even guess what he was about. Above the report of the second shot I heard the yelp of the dog and the barking of its companion. I saw my son running fast, gun at the ready, across the yard, vaulting the fence and into the fields. I watched as he drew, and the cry of the second dog came back to me before the report did. The guineas suddenly found their voices and frantically began their screaming from the high pines where they had apparently fled.

He crossed the fence back toward me, and I saw him eject the unspent shells as he came.

"Got 'em both!" He slammed the back door and set the gun beside it. "I can hear the others over toward the Austins' and in the cemetery."

The wild dogs that roamed the river bottoms were a greater threat to us than any other predator, especially in the spring when the river rose and drove them in to us. Mainly they wanted the calves. It was rare for them to come up so near the house.

"I didn't even see them," I said.

"Saw 'em out of the corner of my eye when the guineas flew up," he responded, settling back on to the counter, wedging his back again into the corner of the over-hanging cabinets. He was as relaxed and placid as he had been ten minutes ago before it all began.

"You'd better clean the gun."

"Not yet. The others will be back to eat these. I'll try to get 'em then." He slid off the counter, our conversation apparently over, and headed back to the shop to help with the shelves.

I couldn't remember when or how it began, this easiness of warfare in him. I could remember that in the second year of our being on The Farm In Lucy, the coyotes came in from the bottoms, and Sam Sr. spent every night for a week hiding in the loft of the barn before he finally managed to kill some and drive the rest of the pack away. But this one had been an infant then, a darling little package of blond good looks still going to grade school in the mornings and bringing me pictures for the refrigerator door in the afternoons. I remembered that he was only mildly curious about what his father was doing in the barn every night. I did recall the morning he came upstairs and, half asleep still, told me, "Daddy got one last night. I heard it yelp," but I never thought of it as more than a child talking about his nighttime.

Maybe his father had taught him to shoot without my knowing. There were the bitter cold nights every winter when the possums came to steal the cat food and warm themselves inside the patio wall. We would hear the kittens cry or the pans rattle against the ice, and one of them, father or son, would get the gun. My chest would hold my breath tightly until the report was over and I knew once more that there had been no ricochet. What I couldn't remember was when, at what point in our lives, Sam Sr. had quit going out with him, or even going at all. When did they, and by what agreement between them, pass the killing on to Sam Jr.?

Perhaps it was that night in the hen house two years before. Bitter cold at midnight when the hens began to scream. They both went, a gun with each of them, and me trailing behind. I got to the gate of the hen yard just in time to hear Sam Sr. shout, "Now! Shoot now!" and to hear the gun.

I heard Sam Jr.'s voice, muffled and coming from inside the hen house, "You okay?"

"Yeah. Thanks, son. He got my sleeve before I saw him." Then, "You're a pretty good marksman in the dark."

"I could see his tail flick. How many chickens did he get?"

"Only two. We can throw them out tomorrow when it's light."

"Okay." And they came out.

Not a word was ever said to me except by Sam Sr., in passing, "Lost two this time. No way in the world to keep coons out."

Later I found the slash in his jacket sleeve and the tear where the coon was clinging when the boy dropped him. Yes, maybe that was the night. After that the guns moved, one by one, down to his bedroom, supposedly so he could keep them oiled and maintained. Even Papaw's ancient rifle went down. I should have known then that guardianship was moving to the boy.

As I stood remembering in my kitchen, both Sams came in the side door together, the smell of the potatoes and my new peas having made its way even to the shop. He was saying to his father, "I probably ought to go down there by the cemetery after lunch and see if they're still there . . . probably be easier to get 'em there than up in the field. These two looked like they were half coyote. If so, they'll run tonight unless I can get them."

"Let's eat first." And they began washing at the sink.

He ate as completely and as loosely as he did everything else, no hurry apparent in his motions, but long before his father and I were done, he nodded his own dismissal and was gone out the door, the gun once more in his hand. I remarked how naturally it sat there, how matter-of-factly he handled it.

"Of course. What else did you expect? He's a boy."

"Doesn't it ever worry you that he kills so quickly?"

"No, only that he might not kill quickly enough. I've seen what a wild dog can do. He never has."

"He saw you the night the coon got your arm."

He looked up, startled that I knew. "You never miss a trick, do you!"

"Somebody had to mend your jacket."

"Well, I'm glad he saw it . . . better my jacket than his hand someday."

Far off to the east of the house I heard the gun.

"Maybe he got one," I said.

"Maybe. Be glad when he's back."

"It does worry you!" I was triumphant at this break in male indifference.

"It should always worry you to send a son against a natural enemy if you've got good sense." He was exasperated with me. "But it'd be a lot worse if he weren't there to send." And he went back to his making and building . . . went back, I must suppose, as God the Father goes back to his in the long, warm days after Easter.

CHAPTER 11

Through the Veil Torn

St. Mark's Day always sticks in my head because of a fluke, a situation that is a bit unfair to poor St. Mark.

Certainly St. Mark has played a rather substantial role in Christian history, particularly in his writing of the earliest Gospel, which bears his name and from which the other three to some extent derived.

Certainly he is impressively commemorated across the world by massive architectural wonders that bear his name and do him homage.

Certainly, as a child, I was charmed completely by the story of his near arrest in the Garden of Gethsemane. Supposedly Mark was the youth whose tunic was ripped off by the arresting soldiers, and he fled the garden naked. When one is a child, stories of nakedness in anyone titillate, and even more so in a saint. Besides, it seemed to me then to have been a better excuse for abandoning the garden than was enjoyed by the rest of the apostles. (In fact, it still comes very close in my mind to being an explanation as well as a pretty sound reason for leaving!) None of these things, however, is why I always remember St. Mark's Day.

Because Easter—or the date for Easter, more correctly—always fluctuates in accord with the date of the first full moon after March 21, it will never fall on the same day in any two consecutive years. Yet the range within which it can come—the earliest possible date and the latest—is fixed forever by that equinox. And Easter can never be later than April 25! St. Mark's Day is Easter's last chance.

As a youngster I somehow convinced myself that the twenty-fifth was called "St. Mark's Day" because it "marked" the last possible date for Easter—and because those in the ancient church were always fond of having fun with things like that. Years of living have not appreciably changed my suspicions, at least not about the church fathers, but they have changed my perception of what St. Mark's marks. St. Mark's Day means the final and irrefutable death of winter for yet another year.

The spring comes so quietly in the country—so without announcement—that I walk into it morning after morning without knowing until abruptly, on some perfectly ordinary day, I think, *It's warm!* and realize that I have already been jacketless and easy in my kingdom for several such mornings. Faith is a bit like that, I suspect, quiet and without announcement till it, too, seeps into our clothing and our decisions and only at the last into our consciousness, till it, too, cuts us loose from chores and clothes and the awkwardness of ice underfoot.

My joy, of course, is in my freedom. The animals are with us again, or I am with them. The fence line no longer holds me separate. I move into their pastures, walking among them as they graze, or they join me in my ramblings down to the pond or off to the close. The world under our feet and about our faces and above our heads is alive again with bees and moths and butterflies and grasshoppers and dragonflies and ladybugs and a myriad of such lives. Their energy charms me, but it is their variety—more infinite than that of the stars—that beguiles me.

It would be so easy, walking these acres, sharing this space, to grow placid and fat of soul—to love these creatures and their haunts beyond their function and place. So beautiful they are to me that only a cross keeps me from the metaphor of pantheism . . .

A cross, a Book, and an Other who, because of the two, lives so close now that I have lost our borders as well as our beginnings. And each Eastertide our conversation is laid aside more completely, more readily, than in the previous spring, while what has been in history and what is always being in nature blend into that sureness of resurrection that contains both.

CHAPTER 12

Patron Saints and a Story of Grief

I was named for my father, whose given name was Philip. Had I belonged to a Catholic family, I doubtless would have claimed St. Philip as my patron saint. As it was, my limited exposure to the saints occurred in the years of my early schooling during and just after the Second World War, when we children were required to read, from time to time, sections of Butler's *Lives of the Saints* for our literature or social studies classes. It was an assignment I always stoutly refused to honor. My Methodist-born father was deathly afraid of "all things papist," as he so charmingly put it, and I was deathly afraid of reading about things that were physically painful. Between the two of us, therefore, we managed to find more than enough reason for me to steer wide of any talk of—or reading about—sanctified pain, and I graduated from high school and later from college without ever once having opened Butler. It was probably one of my more costly mistakes.

As a result, I was ill-prepared many years later for dealing with what was to happen to Sam and me. At two weeks of age, our second son and fifth child died of pneumonia.

Months after the violent passing, still numb and purposeless, we left the other children with our mothers and went off together on a kind of winter retreat or sabbatical in the mountains, hoping to discover there the energy and the perspective that would let us begin again.

It was the third or fourth day of our time there, and I was feeling more at peace than I had for weeks. The afternoon itself was cozily damp, and the mountains around us were glorious in their fog and drizzle. The secondhand bookstore where we were browsing was charming and quiet. A teakettle, if you can believe it, even simmered on the potbellied stove in the back. The whole village, in fact, was straight out of a brochure, but I was greatly in need of clichés. I was even beginning to trust them. Then suddenly, there on the shelf in front of me, was Butler—a bit mildewed, but there. Invulnerable at last, or so I thought, I picked him up and began to read.

I had always known that whatever else saints may be about, they are most certainly about suffering. What I had never known is that saints are those who neither need their pain nor value it nor ask anything of it. Butler's saints asked of misfortune no cosmic meaning and no personal gain. Indeed, as I stood there reading page after page, it was not the denial of pleasure or the pursuit of poverty or the desire for martyrdom (which things I had always assumed marked a saint), but the letting go that seemed to characterize Butler's heroes. It was, as a discovery, a great shock to my new equilibrium, one I deeply resented at the time.

I had discovered that in real pain, and in genuine grief, there was a kind of immunity from more pain or even from much engagement. Having suffered, I felt that I would not have to suffer again for a long, long time—perhaps even for the rest of my life. I had bought my peace the hard way. Even more, because I had hurt and still was hurting, I knew I was alive. I could touch that pain and be reassured by it, could flatter myself that it had some meaning beyond bacteria and medical accident. I even dredged up Aeschylus and persuaded myself that I had indeed gained wisdom through all of this. After all, these were the insights that our friends and family had sent us to the mountains to achieve.

But there was Butler with his tales of men and women who didn't have to hold on to their pain, who didn't need it to buy themselves immunity from life, who didn't find the reassurance of their own worth in it. Why? Butler seemed to be saying that it was because they every one—to a man and to a woman—believed themselves to have already been validated by God's pain; they believed that all those things I was asking of my grief had already been provided by divine grief. They had let go. I could not. It was the first time I had ever understood the necessity for his "Eloi, Eloi, lama sabachthani!" (Mark 15:34).

I put Butler back on the shelf and left the store. It was only ten minutes later, back in our room, that I realized I had also left Sam, but it didn't matter. He took my absentmindedness as a sure sign of returning health, for absentmindedness has always characterized me as surely as better qualities have characterized the saints.

We left the next day. I couldn't bear all that pseudo-Tyrolean resort decor and said so rather forcefully. Sam laughed. It was the first time, I realized, that I had heard him laugh in weeks.

We came back to our lives and our children. In time we found The Farm In Lucy, bought it, and moved here. The ache for the boy who never grew up on it is no bigger and no smaller than it was all those years ago, just quieter and less arrogant—which is as much instruction and relief as any of us has any right to hope for from stories of other people's faith . . . at least in faith's beginning.

CHAPTER 13

Dance of the Fireflies

There are three days in the spring of the church year when, traditionally, believers begged the blessing of God upon earth and its crops. Now, removed as we are from any intimacy with the production of our food, we no longer feel the ancient urgency to *rogare*, as the Latin had it, "to ask or beseech." Yet Rogation Days have stayed on many church calendars. They fall on the Monday, Tuesday, and Wednesday immediately preceding Ascension. Because the Thursday of Ascension is numbered from Easter, and Easter is calculated from the vernal equinox, these three days float, within a limited range of possibilities, in the natural calendar. They almost always, therefore, occur close to, or simultaneous with, that one part of life on our farm that has always commanded my attention— the coming of the fireflies.

The night when the fireflies mate is always preceded by hours of subtle but obvious preparation. In the years when the children were still at home, the afternoon always moved with an unsettling orderliness regardless of how the day itself may have begun. Even if a faint breeze were playing about, no real wind disturbed the waiting grasses. Across the fence line and in the meadow, the assertive green of middle spring would change to a yellow glow under an afternoon sun that invariably was warm but not yet hot. The cows, with a delicacy beyond my understanding, retreated before their usual hour to the feeding lot outside the barn. It was their early going, in fact, that most persuaded me that this was the first of the three nights. The quiet was so soft that even the children would ask, "Is it time?"

The dark comes late in the first days of May. And it comes luminous, like the world of my prayers where no thing is, save *is* itself. The meadow begins to grow indistinct and distant from the kitchen window. I step to the back door and see the first one. It is time.

In a family of many, most things are communal. The coming of the fireflies is not and never was. Whether the children used to watch from other places on the farm, had other secret windows of their own, I never knew. I never asked and was never told. For my own part, I watch from just inside the fence line, sometimes sitting on a stump there, sometimes standing, sometimes resting in the hammock. Wherever I am, I soon forget the what and how of me.

The number of the lights always increases slowly, a few near me, a few over toward Mary's Hill. Rising from the meadow grasses they come in twos and threes and fours. By ten o'clock the meadow as far as one can see is filled with them, the air above the grasses flashing and throbbing with the dance of their passion.

By midnight they are all done. The blanket of lights settles gradually into the grass and finally stops altogether. The next night and the night after that they mate again, but I will not come to watch as I did on that first night. Or if I do, I bring someone with me—Sam, a child, a neighbor—and we lean on the fence rail, chatting as we watch, like spectators at a zoo. Once the process has begun, this copulation for which there is no perceptible schedule but in which all of nature seems to acquiesce, once this is in place, then it becomes just another phenomenon to be mentioned. It is only on this first night of confirmation that the awe hovers, like the lights of the dancing, about me.

The ancient story says that Job bowed down before the whirlwind and out of it heard the voice of his God.

> Where wast thou when I laid the foundations of the earth? declare, if thou hast understanding. . . . who laid the corner stone thereof; When the morning stars sang together, and all the sons of God shouted for joy? Or who shut up the sea with doors, when it brake forth, as if it had issued out of the womb? . . . Hast thou entered into the springs of the sea? or hast thou walked in the search of the depth? Have the gates of death been opened unto thee? or hast thou seen the doors of the shadow of death? . . . declare if thou knowest it all. (Job 38:4, 6–8, 16–18)

The story also says that Job, having heard, answered: "I have heard of thee by the hearing of the ear: but now mine eye seeth thee. Wherefore I abhor myself, and repent in dust and ashes" (Job 42:5–6).

And, alone on this first night of the fireflies and caught in the whirlwind of their lights, I know that Job's story is true. Mine eye seeth thee and I repent before such grandeur.

CHAPTER 14

Ascension Day

According to the New Testament, after Christ was resurrected and at the end of the forty days during which he appeared to many and spoke with his disciples, "while he blessed them, he was parted from them, and carried up into heaven" (Luke 24:51). He ascended into heaven, and the church celebrates this part of Easter season as Ascension Day.

During my own tenth year, however, I wrestled not so much with the miracle of ascension as with the horrible possibility that it, along with resurrection and heaven, was not so desirable after all. The months of my unease began innocuously enough. I simply went with my cousins to see a movie. The problem was the movie. It was Walt Disney's *Fantasia*. Like much of Disney's work, *Fantasia* was, and is, as much for adults as for young children. What it most definitely is *not* for is the human imaginations caught between those two categories.

I can still remember sitting in the old Majestic Theatre that Saturday afternoon and being delighted to the core of my being as the colors and images of the myths I so loved became suddenly animate and visible on the screen before me. I can also remember, alas, the vividness of my shock when, in the movie's closing scenes, Disney's ethereal angel-children began to float spinelessly over misty meadows through banks of white flowers toward a pale opening in a pale sky. What had happened to all the dancing flowers and the silly laughter and the prancing high jinks that had so charmed me for the past hour and a quarter? It was awful. Frame after frame went by, and still there was nothing even remotely colorful or even halfway compelling on the entire screen. Dying seemed to involve ascending into nowhere, and ascending seemed to require more boneless, bodiless wafting. I couldn't accept the notion that Disney was a liar, but neither could I tolerate the notion that his take on the hereafter was true.

While the adults around me wept more and more audibly, they also seemed more wrapped in sadness than horror. In fact, as I tried to read their faces in the

flickering half-light produced by Disney's flowery meadows, I could discern not one adult who looked anything
less than transported into a maudlin peace. As for my
two cousins, they were both totally unconcerned with
the dying, ascending, and wafting, being instead totally
concerned with splitting the last of our popcorn equi-
tably between them. *Maybe*, I thought, the adult sniffling
rising all the while to a crescendo as the procession on
the screen grew ever fainter and silverier, *maybe this is
only how it is if you die old. But if you died young, then maybe
it's still colors and dancing and laughing.*

I decided to set my mind to considering this solution
in greater depth, which was not hard to do, because my
grandmother was dying of cancer that summer. Both her
progress and her color resembled the Disney progression
across the misty meadows far more than they resembled
the brilliance of jonquils and tulips recycling back into
foliage and bulbs. Sure enough, Grandmother died the
following October, and the grown-ups around me put
her in a white casket, surrounded her with unnaturally
white flowers, and buried her during a funeral to which
everyone except me wore black. I wore red.

My churching, up to this point, had been arduous
and deliberate. In direct proportion to that adult effort

and like all children, I had offered the opposition of polite disinterest and intellectual disengagement. But with the funeral and *Fantasia* coming up on each other so close like that, even a strong will had difficulty ignoring the obvious.

I was crossing through the hallway that led from the narthex to the Sunday school rooms one bleak Sunday morning in late November several weeks after Grandmother's funeral when I chanced to look up at the stained-glass window that rose two stories high behind the stairwell and illuminated the whole passageway. For the first time I perceived that the figure in the window was Christ's—his feet, on the bottom floor, floated above the haloed heads of the apostles. His arms were raised in blessing over the landing, while his head moved steadily upward toward the second-story ceiling and the hole of faded, cream glass in the curved arch of the window. I knew I was in trouble. I raced around the stair to the base of the window, climbed up on the window seat, and with difficulty, read the words, "Ascension Day—Gift of Dr. and Mrs. ——, May, 1929," on the brass plaque. Walt Disney *was* right! I never made it to Sunday school that day. In fact, I don't even remember making it to services. My fears had been confirmed.

If this pale, too-calm Christ was any indication, heaven was strictly Cream of Wheat and Ovaltine.

Given that ominous revelation and allowing for the fact that I had grown too old to feel comfortable with Easter baskets and somewhat suspect bunnies, I faced the coming spring and Holy Week with less enthusiasm than any child in my whole circle of cousins and acquaintances. In fact, I probably endured the most miserable Lent that any child has ever passed through— far worse, certainly, than what penitence itself would ever create for me later in adulthood. For distress of soul and mind, nothing could ever again approach the rigors of my tenth year. I had somehow made it, unasked, into existence, and I really didn't mind that. Life—at least my life—was not bad and seemed, as I watched the adult world around me, to offer several chances of getting better. What had me by the hair of my spiritual head, on that Lent, was that I could not find any way out of existence that was acceptable, that did not, with its awesome pallor, suck the joy out of the young days I had in hand.

We made it through Easter. I dyed eggs because everyone else did (even my father helping with the last batch) and because I loved beyond all other things at

Easter the way my mother pickled beets on Easter Monday and then added the shelled and abandoned Easter eggs to the juice. The sight of the purplish red eggs and the tart, cold beets on my Easter Monday dinner plate was the apex of the holiday for me every year, and I was not to be robbed of that pleasure even in this tenth and most dreadful year.

Ascension Day came and I shuddered in the warm, sunset light that streamed through the stairwell Christ, but either no one saw me standing there, or no one cared. And there, all alone in that corridor, the sounds of the congregation gathering beyond me for Ascension services and the pale Christ with his pale heaven floating above me, I experienced that shattering and totally engaging rebellion that is the beginning of mature religion, the first sign of honest grace. In later life I would regard the distress of those moments and of that Lent in general as the labor pains of the soul, which always precede new instruction and new stages of union. But there in that hallway and then in that young body, I had no previous experience by which to gauge what was happening to me. I only knew that the stained-glass Christ and the Walt Disney heaven were the same and that they both were a grown-up lie. I knew that such a heaven was not worth living for, not worth creating creation for, even. That God's death, the only one we could see for ourselves anyway, was the spring's blazing passage from pastel to green.

And so I ran frantically out of that hallway and into the churchyard, throwing myself down on the new grass, its green staining my clothes and its crushed blades filling my nose with the bitter odor of spilled sap. There was real death to be part of every spring, and I was rolling in it, humming and throwing tufts of grass into the air and being ten again for the first time in weeks.

Pentecost came, of course, and tongues of gorgeous red fire blazed at me from the church bulletin, from the wall posters in the Sunday school rooms, from the hangings behind the altar. Red leaves pulled from the undersides of rosebushes decorated the altar, and only the baptismal candidates wore white. In another week the trappings were all changed to comfortable, brilliant green and reassuringly stayed that way until the anniversary of Grandmother's death, when I was freshly turned eleven and when our pastor preached on the dying of the church year, the folding away of the green to make way for Advent.

Afterward, being eleven, I walked, rather than ran, out to the hallway at the end of the narthex. The Christ in the window was still pale, but I could have sworn, in that late November light, that he winked at me from his place above the landing. Whether he did or not really doesn't matter, of course. What matters is that at eleven I thought he did, and it was the beginning of a long and consuming relationship between the two of us.

Epilogue

Of the three Christian seasons, Easter is the oldest and the most sacred. It is also the most tightly focused. Technically it is itself composed of Lent, Easter, and the Great Fifty Days, which include Ascensiontide. It begins, for the devout, with what many folk used to call pre-Lent, but at a popular and widely understood level, it begins with Mardi Gras and Ash Wednesday. It ends with the Feast of Pentecost on the fiftieth and last day of the Great Fifty Days.

In the beginning of things, the Great Fifty Days, which stretch from Easter morning to Pentecost, were the holy part of the season. With the coming of a number of social and cultural changes during the postmedieval ages and especially with the coming of the church to America, emphasis shifted for several centuries to Lent. Lent had—and has—the singular advantage of giving people something to *do*, a very important characteristic for a religion that was passing from its infancy into its adolescence, and even more important for one that was passing into the hands of a merchant class and an urbanized culture. As Christianity and/or America have matured, there has been a gradual tendency to return to the old ways, to the Great Fifty Days as the center of Eastertide. It is a shift that most of us probably welcome, to the extent that we have even noticed it, and it in no way detracts from the forty days of Lenten preparation. What this change of emphasis does do, however, is make the spring of the church a long holy season, taking it from Fat Tuesday for ninety-seven days (or a full calendar quarter) to Pentecost and the beginning of Ordinary Time.

It would be wrong of me to leave this book or to come away from these pages without saying one last time that they are, when all is finally said and done, about Easter. And that Easter is the straight stuff, straight, hard-core Christianity.

We can all enjoy Christmas because commercialization and secular culture have given it a kind of spiritual distance for many of us. We have managed, in this world of many faiths and careless tolerations, to agree on a Lupercalia or Saturnalia in which we celebrate and exercise that which is most intellectually acceptable to our common definition of what humankind at its best should be. In proclaiming universal love and possible peace to each other for a few hours of the midwinter, we absolve ourselves of the burden of hopelessness and perhaps of incipient godlessness, for Christmas can be shared by Christian, semi-Christian, and flagrant pagan alike, all of us agreeing in its moral stances and cultural postures. Thank God we have such a day once a year.

But Easter is not so tractable. It is not about morality and the common good. It cannot be shared with a Muslim fellow or a Jewish neighbor or a quasi-Christian. Nor can one write about Easter with the philosophical insights and enlightened self-interest of the professional moralist. Easter strips all of that away, and one is left naked of abilities, cleverness, and dignity. One is left, ultimately, with Easter. There is the mystery of eating this God, of incorporating him into oneself, body into body—a mystery so dark as to lie beyond the memory of humankind and beyond the reach of human poetry.

> Verily, verily, I say unto you, Except ye eat the flesh of the Son of man, and drink his blood, ye have no life in you. Whoso eateth my flesh, and

> drinketh my blood, hath eternal life; . . . He that
> eateth my flesh, and drinketh my blood,
> dwelleth in me, and I in him. As the living
> Father hath sent me, and I live by the Father: so
> he that eateth me, even he shall live by me.
> (John 6:53–54, 56–57)

There is the mystery of the many realities, the lifting, however briefly, of the veil. "I beheld Satan as lightning fall from heaven" (Luke 10:18). And in the garden, as reckless Peter comes to his defense, "Thinkest thou that I cannot now pray to my Father, and he shall presently give me more than twelve legions of angels?" (Matthew 26:53).

There is the mystery of death briefly seen, the veil lifted here and there, in the three years Christ spent with his chosen twelve disciples. But now, in this week of their ending, it is torn forever, leaving eleven men, five mourning women, one Roman centurion, and all of history with more than it can scarcely summon the courage to acknowledge, much less act upon. Had Christ not already told them many times: "Your father Abraham rejoiced to see my day: and he saw it, and was glad. . . . Verily, verily, I say unto you, Before Abraham was, I am" (John 8:56, 58)? "Now that the dead are raised, even Moses shewed at the bush, when he calleth the Lord the God of Abraham, and the God of Isaac, and the God of Jacob. For he is not a God of the dead, but of the living: for all live unto him" (Luke 20:37–38). And in his death cry amidst the tearing of the temple veil and the quaking of the earth, "the graves were opened; and many bodies of the saints which slept arose, And came out of the graves after his resurrection, and went into the holy city, and appeared unto many" (Matthew 27:52–53). Followed less than three days later with "Touch me not; for I am not yet ascended to my Father: but go to my brethren, and say unto them, I ascend unto my Father, and your Father; and to my God, and your God" (John 20:17).

There is the mystery that, death having been penetrated and passage having been given through communion, God, the divine Self, chooses to move into us. "And I will pray the Father, and he shall give you another Comforter, that he may abide with you for ever; Even the Spirit of truth; . . . ye know him; for he dwelleth with you, and shall be in you" (John 14:16–17).

Then there is the final mystery, the one greater for me even than death itself. There is the mystery that this is God . . . that this Jew roaming the streets cursing fig trees and raging at money changers, healing children and feeding hundreds, calming winds and stopping storms, casting out devils and speaking to evil spirits is God . . . that this is what we claim to worship. That opening my mouth to receive the elements, bowing my head to pray, and lifting my children up for baptism, I claim all of this as God, as that of which I am, as process and cause and purpose, as mystery and master. To the extent that what I am can translate itself into words that my mind can render to my fellows, this is what I am by virtue of grace and those very elements. This is Christianity, and it brooks little argument.